To

R. Micki

With love and.

great affection

Judy Stevens

Living Well,

Dying Well

Fielding University Press is an imprint of Fielding Graduate University.
Its objective is to advance the research and scholarship of Fielding faculty, students and
alumni around the world, using a variety of publishing platforms.

For more information, please contact Fielding University Press, attn. Dr. Jean-Pierre
Isbouts, via email to jisbouts@fielding.edu, or via postal mail to Fielding Graduate University, 2020 De la Vina Street, Santa Barbara, CA 93105.
On the web: www.fielding.edu/universitypress.

Library of Congress Cataloging-in-Publication data
Living Well, Dying Well
1. Social Sciences – End of life considerations.

Living Well, Dying Well

A practical guide to choices, costs, and consequences

Judith Stevens-Long, PhD

Dohrea Bardell, PhD

This Page intentionally left blank

TABLE OF CONTENTS

Part Four: What happens after we die?

Author's Preface

By the time I joined Hospice of Santa Barbara two years ago, I had begun to develop my ideas for this book, and I knew it would be no fun at all to do it alone. You definitely need someone to talk to when you undertake a book about death and dying. No one wants to talk about it as a part of the dinner conversation, and even your best friends start to wonder if you aren't a bit nuts to be thinking about it all the time. So, I asked Dohrea if she would like to co-author this book. I had been writing and thinking about the subject for a long time, having reviewed the literature every few years through four editions of *Adult Life*, my textbook on adult development.

I'm sure Dohrea was taken aback by the offer. She hadn't been thinking about death at all! She had just finished her dissertation, in which she had developed a theory of peace based on the work of Immanuel Kant. After a moment or two of shock and wonder, she agreed, a great relief to me. I was on her dissertation committee, and I knew she was one of the most careful and thorough researchers I had the pleasure of knowing. So, I asked her to shepherd the chapters that needed the latest, most up-to-date information: chronic illness; funerals; and near-death-experience. Her chapters are the ones in which you will find the latest information on caring for our health and the health of our planet—in other words, living well.

Over the past year or two, both of us have had experiences with death that have contributed to our understanding of how life and death are interrelated. We've wished that the people we knew would take better care of themselves, talk to us more frankly, and reach out to us more often. We've had some unusual experiences tied to our journey. Sometimes we wondered whether our work was attracting end-of-life experiences, or if we were just more sensitive to the possibilities. Immersing yourself in how people live the last years or months of their lives is not particularly easy, but like so many hard things in life, it gives you a deeper appreciation of beauty and joy, the importance of living well to the end, and the possibility of personal growth in the last phases of life.

We have had enormous support from our husbands, Larry and Seann, and friends, especially Dr. Steven Jones, Dr. Steven Morton, Sudi Staub, Patrice Rosenthal, Katrina Rogers, and Daneen Skube, who were all available to talk about our project even over lunch or dinner. Special thanks to the folks at Hospice of Santa Barbara, the people who contributed the stories you'll find in the boxes inside and, of course Jean-Pierre Isbouts, our editor, who accepted this project without hesitation and has been helpful and supportive of our work from the beginning.

In memory of Donald Burdick

1971-2018

INTRODUCTION

We hope this book will help you, the reader, learn about how the institutions of death and dying are changing in the United States. We believe the U.S., with a big push from the baby boomers, is moving toward a culture that provides a greater array of choices for positive ways to both live and die in the final phase of your life. Today, people are living for many years with the acute awareness that their remaining time is limited, inspiring them to find new ways to create joy and comfort until the very last moment of life. This book contains all the information you need to make the best decisions for ensuring that the last years of your life, or the life of someone you love, will be as satisfying, comfortable, and even as productive as possible.

The first section of this book is devoted to the American quest for a better quality of life at the end of life. We discuss the emerging trends that are changing the face of dying in the twenty-first century. Increasingly, medicine is putting the decisions about how long we will live and how we will die in our own hands. There is a plethora of new ideas about self-care, living arrangements, medical options, and personal relationships at the end of life. Understanding the range of choices that are available can help you make the best decisions for yourself, for your family, and for the people under your care. We believe the last years of the baby boomers are likely to revolutionize the concluding years of life for generations to come, in ways that make those years both more manageable and more meaningful.

In the first section, we also look at how death itself has been redefined by the medical establishment over the past few decades and at the possibilities and problems emerging from new technologies. We outline the major causes of death in America and the likely course of the most common fatal diseases, in order to help you better understand and make decisions about the issues that can come up at the end of life.

In the second section, we cover the interpersonal aspects of the decisions you might need to make at the end of life. How do you start a conversation about dying with your spouse, your child, or your parent? How can you instill the end of life with the meaning and values that are important to you and your family? What do you want, for yourself and the people you care about, in the ending phase of life? How will you honor the desires and values of those you'll need to care for? What do you want people to know about who you are and what you want as you move through your final years?

We also cover nitty-gritty issues. What is a *natural death* and what are the options that this approach to death can offer you? How do you make your wishes clear to your family, friends, and healthcare providers? Are there stages or phases in the last part of life? How does personality fit into our understanding of the ways people manage these years? We walk you through the forms, the legalities, and the blind alleys, and through the new paths that are available to the dying and their families. We describe the opinions of the experts and the research on how people actually live out the eleventh hour of their lives.

Those who care for the dying are accepting an often daunting task. We outline all the issues they face. What are the major stresses and what are the ultimate benefits of helping someone through a chronic illness or a terminal disease? What resources are available? What can you do to make this experience as positive as possible for your family and friends and for you? We also address how caretakers can attend to their own needs while they're giving so much to those who need their care.

A multitude of choices can arise in the final months and days of your life. We review the research about what the important factors are when choosing between hospice and a hospital, what it means to invite palliative care, and what's involved in living life at home until the end. We discuss the opportunities for growth, joy, and comfort, as well as how people manage their anxiety and pain. We outline the course of events likely to accompany the various ways people live when they're about to die.

We will cover how to have a conversation with family and friends, what kinds of documents need to be on file, where to file them, and the options that are emerging in funeral planning (and costs). We will describe

10

how various kinds of dying play out in the last stage of life and tackle how to talk to a person who is dying.

We will also address various kinds of bereavement following a) a peaceful, predictable death of an elderly parent or friend, b) the complicated issues that accompany a traumatic death, such as from suicide or natural disaster, and c) a significantly premature death, such as that of a child or adolescent. There is a huge, well-researched literature on death and dying in the United States, and we'll break it all down as best we can, so you know what to expect and whether there is something you can do to make it less difficult, and more meaningful, for both the dying and the survivors.

In the final chapters of this book, we discuss what is known about surviving the death of another. We look at new ways you can celebrate the life and mourn the death of someone you care about. We discuss what grief is and how it's different from mourning. We talk about cultural differences, the rituals and rites, and the opportunities for supporting others who are facing the death of someone they love. We include what different traditions teach about the handling of the body, what it costs to purchase a funeral, what to expect as a survivor, and what to provide when you want to help a friend.

We also look at the some of the great mysteries of dying. What is a deathbed vision or a near-death experience? Is it just a hallucination, or is it an experience of something real? What does it tell us about living? Yes, we tackle the question of what encountering death can do for the living. We describe *post-traumatic growth*, the psychological growth that people report in the aftermath of traumatic experiences. We talk about the possibility of renewal and the infusion of new meaning that the difficult experiences in your life can generate. This book is about choice. Its focus is on death and dying, but ultimately, it's about life.

Much of what we report in this book is derived from the latest journal articles and handbooks on death and dying, as well as from government reports from the Centers for Disease Control; the National Institute of Health; and the National Academies of Science, Engineering, and Medicine. In particular, the *Handbook of Thanatology* (thanatology is the study of death and dying) and the 600-page report of the Institute of Medicine of the National Academies (2015), called *Dying in America*, were useful in preparing this guide. Both of these important resources begin, as do we, with a description of what death and dying looked like when we began to think, research, and write about the subject in 1969, after Elizabeth Kübler-Ross published her famous ideas about the stages of dying.

We designed this book so you can read it out of sequence: you can start anywhere. Begin with the topic that's most important to you at this moment. Each chapter is short, and none of the information in a chapter depends on reading the chapter before. You can use the Table of Contents to move from topic to topic to find the help you need right now. You might not want to start with a description of the general systems that societies have evolved for dealing with their dying. Maybe all you need to know this minute is what palliative care has to offer or how to choose a hospice or plan a funeral. You may want to figure out what to say to a loved one who's just learned they have a terminal or life-threatening illness. Feel free to use this book in whatever way best suits your emerging needs and immediate curiosities.

The end of life holds hidden possibilities. It's not just a dead end, nor does it have to be filled with unbearable sorrow. This book points the way to how we can live with love and dignity to the very end.

JUDITH STEVENS-LONG AND DOHREA BARDELL

PART ONE

How the system is changing:

Living and dying in America

CHAPTER 1

THE 20TH CENTURY MODEL: CONVENTIONAL END-OF-LIFE CHOICES

". . .for it might end, you know," said Alice, "in my going out alto-gether, like a candle. I wonder what I should be like then." And she tried to fancy what the flame of a candle is like after the candle is blown out, for she could not remember ever having seen such a thing."

Lewis Carroll

This line from *Alice in Wonderland*, written in 1865, captures the major concern of this book: the journey from life to death. Many experts argue that the experiences of Alice are understood best as a story about death, from falling down the rabbit hole to the trial in front of the Queen of Hearts. Of course, Carroll never directly mentions death and so, like most twentieth-century Americans, Alice never says a word about it either.

We don't know what it means to be dead, which, all by itself, provokes anxiety. Most of us do what we can to avoid what causes us anxiety and, for at least the last 150 years, Americans have been keeping death at a decent distance. In our modern cities and nuclear families, we seldom encounter death. Since we don't live in extended families, elderly relatives often live alone and are likely to die in hospitals or nursing homes. The death of a pet is about as close as we get. We don't even use words like *death* or *dying*. We say people "pass away" or "go to a better place," though we don't really know much about that place. We have a "bucket list," not "things to do before we die."

To begin our story, let's start with how things stood in the dying business in 1969—not so long ago, really. All of the baby boomers had been born by 1969 and Gen X was coming along. Criticism of the funeral industry, however, had begun before Kübler-Ross, with the 1965 publication of a book by sociologist Jessica Mitford. In *The American Way of Death*, she argued that the death trade had become a profit-oriented business that thrived on the inability of Americans to face death or see it as a natural part of life.

Mitford pointed out that embalming and the use of cosmetics had been practiced in only two societies over the course of history, in ancient Egypt (see box) and in twentieth-century America. The use of metal caskets was almost unknown outside of the United States, much less the expensive, ornate coffins that lined the walls of funeral-parlor showrooms by the 1960s. Mitford believed that Americans spent ridiculous amounts of money trying to fulfill an irrational desire to preserve the body, reinforcing the fantasy that the person is somehow "only gone away," as one popular greeting card read.

Dying Well In Ancient Egypt

Perhaps the zenith of funerary obsession in all of history occurred in the Golden Age of Egyptian culture. The earliest versions of *The Egyptian Book of the Dead*, a guide to the underworld, dated from 1500 BCE, near the beginning of the Golden Age. *The Book of the Dead* is a collection of magic spells or formulas that served to prepare the reader for the challenges of the afterlife. Papyrus was plentiful in Egypt during this era, and thousands of copies of the book were produced. In fact, preparation for death and the afterlife consumed a significant portion of the Egyptian economy, perhaps as much as 70%, as well as most of the adult life of a wealthy person.

Egyptians believed that the afterlife called for many things found in everyday life, such as a residence, food and drink, tools, weapons, and the attention of the living. A priest had to be secured to perform appropriate rituals, and servants were paid to maintain the tomb along with its contents. The afterlife held a complex and, to the twenty-first-century mind, largely incoherent set of dangers and challenges, including an almost continual battle against total annihilation. One might be assaulted by a god or a serpent or lose an important bodily function, such as talking or breathing, which would still cause problems even though one was dead. Knowing the spells outlined in *The Book of the Dead*, including the names of the many gods and their animals, could allow one to continue to fight another day. Most of an Egyptian's life might be lived awash with anxiety and dread, preparing for this eternal nastiness.

By the end of the twentieth century, the average cost of funeral services stood at $1,500 ($4,500 in today's dollars), depending on the location of the internment site. Today, that figure is twice that. By the time a family buys a burial plot, orders flowers, rents a chapel, hires a musician, and pays an honorarium to the clergyman, a funeral has become the third most expensive purchase a family will ever make. Despite all of this effort and expense, however, very little was actually known in 1969 about what kinds of rituals and services might be helpful to the bereaved. More often than not, survivors decided what was to be done and, without information, people are most likely to choose what is familiar, whether it makes any sense or not.

Forest Lawn Cemetery in Glendale, California, exemplifies how the funeral industry operated in the last part of the century. A minimal funeral with burial, endowment care, a sectional concrete box (required to keep the earth from falling into a grave containing a casket), internment, and recording could be purchased for $1,700 in 1980. The package included a simple casket. Thousands of people are interred at the Glendale park (they call it a park, not a cemetery), and Forest Lawn owns five other California locations. In a visit to Forest Lawn in the eighties, you would find that the park did not have dirt. It had "earth." The walls of the counseling rooms, where families meet with funeral directors, were painted a soft green, and a slight floral scent floated through the premises. Forest Lawn's widespread radio advertising suggested that the major reason people overspent on funerals was a lack of preplanning. The salespeople at Forest Lawn argued that preplanning protected survivors from impulse buying. Many critics, however, argued that it is difficult to control overspending when a funeral like the one at Forest Lawn is the predominant ritual available to families.

Other critics have argued that American funeral practices, including the Forest Lawn funeral, were (and still are) too brief and informal. Americans are not required to wear special garb, as do the bereaved in other cultures. Survivors do not observe any specified period of mourning; you may continue your social calendar without taking a moment. It was believed by some that this obvious lack of ritual has made it more likely that bereaved survivors will respond to death in maladaptive ways. Despite the cost and effort behind elaborate funerals, survivors often experienced embalming, hauling big floral arrangements home after the service, and other practices as a source of distress rather than comfort.

Early research in the seventies and eighties revealed that most people had unrealistic ideas about dying. For example, when college students imagined their deathbed scene, they would consistently imagine they would be quite old, at least 90, maybe 100. They talked about how their death would be peaceful and quick. They would die at home and know beforehand, so that they could call their friends and relatives to come and say goodbye. The final moment, they imagined, would then come quickly, perhaps while sleeping, and survivors would have a big party instead of a funeral. The chances that something like this would happen were close to zero. In the late twentieth century, about 80% of all deaths occurred in hospitals, nursing homes, or retirement facilities. Of the rest, some were accidental or sudden. Though some people did die at home naturally, resources for taking care of the terminally ill at home were limited and costly. This scenario is still unlikely for, as we shall see, most elderly people today will die of multiple chronic conditions that may last for months or even years. Before they die, they will require long-term care, with several admissions to emergency rooms.

Many psychiatrists contend that since industrial society is organized around the nuclear family, death is experienced more intensely by survivors than in places where people live in extended families or intricate kinship systems. An individual death is less important in a complicated, fast-moving society; therefore, complex societies offer few customs and rituals for the bereaved. In fact, in the twentieth century, there was little information about either the dying process or responses to death. Early in the century, psychologists had begun to think of themselves as natural scientists. As a consequence, they excluded the study of events that could not be objectively measured, and they were not inclined to address the substantial problem of defining death, much less dying.

Death Anxiety

For most of the twentieth century, death was an uncomfortable, unpleasant, and taboo subject. Nobody wanted to talk about it, research it, or deal with the dying. In the Western world, death is incompatible with the dominant value system. Mainstream Americans see death as a defeat. In death, one loses the ability to produce, to achieve, or to have a dream for the future. Most Americans fear dying; yet this fear is not universal. In fact, it may be a by-product of learning to be an independent, productive American.

It isn't possible to fear death based on our personal experience, since we have no personal experience of it (that we know of). We do experience the death of other people, though, and it's often hard for us to distinguish what the dying feel and think from what we feel and think about dying. We have no idea how it feels to be dead, but we associate death with loss and the attendant feelings of grief and anxiety. Furthermore, dead people don't move around a lot, and most Americans fear immobility and inactivity. It's considered quite upsetting to relieve elderly people of their car keys, just to note one common issue around mobility.

Death is not, however, experienced as threatening in all societies. This has been frequently illustrated by cross-cultural research across the globe. For example, although they don't have strong feelings about immortality, members of many Polynesian kin groups believe that death must be pleasant, given that the dead no longer have any responsibility and don't have to work. Polynesian culture doesn't foster a strong need for achievement, and most members of a kin group have many important emotional relationships. Polynesians do not report feelings of separation anxiety or fears of abandonment, common feelings among Americans. Other studies show that death anxiety among Americans is strongly influenced by relationships between family members. Mother/daughter and father/son pairs have similar scores on measures of anxiety, as do spouses. These data imply that death anxiety is learned in the family and that it might be alleviated by therapies based on learning theory.

Another explanation for death anxiety among mainstream Americans has been offered by existential psychologists. They argue that, in the nuclear age, people experience death anxiety because life itself is experienced as meaningless. These writers maintain that, where religious beliefs are waning and no one is certain humankind can prevent a nuclear holocaust, death anxiety becomes so strong people need to deny the inevitability of death. People become unable to consider or encounter death because it is viewed as a void, an end to existence. Robert Lifton, a prolific writer on meaning in modern society, has proposed that the possibility of Armageddon creates an indelible image of death as a senseless tragedy rather than a fitting end to life. He was influenced by the stories of those who were interred in German concentration camps and those who survived either the bombing of Hiroshima or the war in Vietnam. In *Living and Dying*, he described five themes he found to be common in all modern cultures:

The death imprint: Survivors report vivid, indelible images of death as grotesque and absurd.

Death guilt: Survivors experience guilt because they were spared. Such guilt is a product of the vulnerability and helplessness that arise when it is impossible to act or even feel appropriately.

Psychological numbing: Suriviors experience a paralysis of the mind in moments of horror, perhaps as an adaptive response to the intensity of feelings caused by such great tragedy.

Suspicion of nurturance: Survivors often resent any offer of help. This may happen because they take it as a sign of weakness or because they are in so much conflict about accepting the horror as reality.

Struggle for meaning: Survivors often spend much of the rest of their lives trying to make sense of and produce meaning from their experience. They may take up a mission that expresses their mourning for those who died. An example is found in the creation of Mothers Against Drunk Driving (MADD).

Lifton believed that these five themes drive an emotional denial of the reality of death. Death and dying become taboo when they rob life of its meaning. This is a hard proposition to research. Since denying is an unconscious process, we are unaware of our denial of feelings. People cannot report things they are unaware of; survey research in the seventies and eighties showed that only 10 to 25% of the population reported that death was an important source of fear in their daily lives. This research also showed, however, that most Americans do believe in some form of social immortality. They believed either that they would be remembered for their achievements or that having descendants would allow them to "live on." The media and our funeral rites reinforce this belief with phrases like "He will always be remembered for...." This belief is inconsistent with the fear that our species will be obliterated by a nuclear war.

Research also demonstrated that most Americans see nuclear weapons as protection, not as a source of grave anxiety, and find it difficult to imagine their own death, much less the death of the species. Very few Americans spend much time thinking or talking about death. Because most people expect to live well into old age, dying is seen as a task reserved for the elderly while the rest of us are supported in our evasion of its inevitability. There is also evidence that older peole are not as anxious about death and dying as the young. In the late eighties, a large number of studies was designed to explore the phenomenon of death anxiety. Gender differences were found. Women experienced more anxiety than did men. Anxiety among healthcare professionals was higher than among the general population, interfering with their ability to relate to dying patients, a subject to which we shall return.

Mutual Pretense

It is rather peculiar that, although a number of studies focused on death anxiety during this era, few researchers seem to have interviewed dying people. One exception stands out, however. In a 1965 study called *Awareness of Dying*, the authors report that dying people and those who care for them tended to enter a state called "mutual pretense." Fifty years ago, people were often not told directly that they were dying and had to test their suspicions with medical staff and family. In response to questions, family members would try to protect themselves with the idea that the patient still had a chance of recovery, and the patient often colluded in this strategy. Healthcare providers would join in this fiction as well and, in fact, as many as a quarter of terminally ill patients in this study never accepted the notion that they were dying at all.

At the same time the pretense was being played out, however, dying people still had to settle unfinished business, manage strained relationships, and retain their composure. The dying were expected to handle their situation with grace and dignity and simultaneously pretend that it was not happening. Since no one talked about dying, everyone in this complex arrangement had a different level of knowledge, from full knowing, to suspicion, to complete ignorance. In such circumstances, denial and acceptance alternate, not only in the person who is dying but also in the whole social network around the person which, as one might imagine, makes functioning well more difficult for everyone.

In fact, there was a heated debate at the time about how much a dying person should be told. Medical caregivers had become the core members of the death system, tasked with delivering both diagnosis and prognosis. Because dying people were most often hospitalized or tucked away in nursing homes, doctors and nurses frequently had to deal not only with the physical symptoms of patients but with their feelings as well.

Anxiety and Caregivers

Unfortunately, most medical caregivers are poorly prepared for this aspect of their role. Trying to save lives, they often experience a patient's death as a personal and professional failure and therefore have a difficult time establishing the right approach to the patient as a peron. If they define their task as helping and curing, they often experience confusion, guilt, and defensiveness when it becomes clear that a cure is not possible. Moreover, people who are trained to save lives, such as doctors, nurses, and first responders, often have a stronger fear of death than other people.

Medical caregivers don't often have the luxury of grief. Once they hand the patient a terminal diagnosis, patients and their families often begin to grieve, feeling shock and anger, depression and guilt, self-recrimination, and the need to resolve unfinished business with the dying. As a consequence, many families accept a patient's death better than the medical staff does. At times, when the family's grief work is done, the family may withdraw from the patient, just as the staff is beginning to experience and express their own sorrow. Hostilities can break out, and, of course, such conflict increases the stress on everyone.

In hospitals, when intense emotions arise, patients and families can be controlled with drugs. The trade-off for such control means that, while there is less personal discomfort, there is also less attention to the emotional and social needs of the dying. When denial is the operative response, efforts to evade recognition of the patient's dying can result in the treating professionals becoming more impersonal and less capable of seeing the uniqueness of each patient. All in all, hospitals can be inhospitable places to die.

By the seventies and eighties, it was becoming clear that something had to change. For one thing, over the course of the previous hundred years, the average human lifespan had increased from 47 to 79 years. Before 1900, the normal life span had changed very little for hundreds of years. In the early part of the century, people died of infectious diseases such as syphillis, typhoid, tuberculosis, diphtheria, or pneumonia. Infectious diseases come on suddenly and, if the person is going to die, he or she dies fairly quickly. As the century came to an end, most people were dying of chronic illnesses such as heart disease, cancer, or stroke. When these diseases are terminal, they often lead to a period between diagnosis and death that can last for months or even years. In addition, many people died in infancy or childhood 100 years ago. Today, nearly 75% of all deaths in the United States occur among people over the age of 65. And, as you can see in Figure 1.1, nearly 40% of adults over the age of 75 have been diagnosed with three or more chronic conditions, except for individuals with the highest incomes; even among the wealthy, more than 30% suffer from three or more chronic diseases. The conditions represented in this figure are hypertension, heart disease, stroke, emphysema, diabetes, cancer, arthritis, and asthma.

Figure 1.1

Prevalence of two or more of nine selected chronic conditions among adults aged 45 and over, by age and percentage of poverty level: United States, 1999-2000 and 2000-2010.

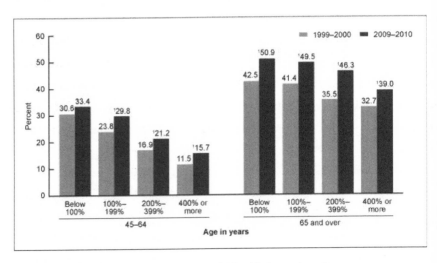

Source: CDC/NCHS, National Health Interview Survey

Chronic Illness and the System of Care

These data have a variety of implications for where we stand now. A significant increase in the number of elderly who are suffering from chronic illness means a significant increase in the number of people with mental and cognitive dysfunction and physical disabilities. Most of the money spent on health care in the United States is spent in the last few years of a life when people also need care outside of a hospital setting, either at home or in a nursing or retirement facility.

Because extended families no longer live together, if a dying person is to be accommodated at home, fewer people are available to participate in that care. Often, home is not an option as there is no one there or nearby to help, so institutionalization is required. When there is a medical emergency, the patient must be ferried to a hospital or medical facility where machines may prolong life by monitoring biological functions, cleaning blood and urine, and even restarting the heart. Every possible resource may be brought to bear in an effort to prolong life. To some, this seems like a prolongation of dying, not living.

Whereas care and comfort were once a burden shared by family, friends, and neighbors, now it either becomes the responsibility of a small circle of close relatives or it falls on the shoulders of a lone spouse or child. This is another way that death becomes invisible to the rest of us. If we don't have to help, we can continue to deny not just the importance of dying, but maybe even its existence. We can avoid seeing death, talking about it, or thinking about it if we are not a member of the inner circle. It's not surprising, then, that people have no idea what to say or do when they hear that a friend or colleague is dying.

In his book, *The Hour of Our Death*, Philippe Ariés argues that not only have the dying become invisible, so have the bereaved. The denial of death leads to the denial of bereavement as well. We know how to handle neither the dying nor their survivors. We see mourning as morbid. Memorial services, scheduled weeks after the death so survivors can become more composed, are becoming increasingly common. With the popularity of the memorial service (and of cremation), the idea of displaying a dead body at a funeral can cause much anxiety and distress and may even be seen as grotesque. Weeping families, especially widows and widowers, are left to struggle by themselves through the days before the memorial and afterward are abandoned again. Once either type of service is over, the needs of the bereaved may be ignored. They must, it is said, learn to live without the deceased.

Ariés also argues that a serious illness is often treated as an indecency and usually no attempt is made to keep a patient at home. Hospitals are crowded with the very old, the incurable, and the dying. Death is locked away in an institution and rarely treated as a natural, necessary phenomenon. When it happens, it must not interrupt the business of the hospital. Most often, patients are not even permitted to die in hospitals at all. Once a patient refuses further treatment, the patient must be moved from the hospital, often before the day is out. Insurance will not pay for a day when the patient does not receive treatment, even though the treatment may be useless.

Attitudes Toward Death

Ariés goes on to point out that a good death today is a death that gives no warning. A good death is one that happens while a person is unconscious. "She died peacefully, in her sleep," is the ideal report. A good death can, therefore, be insured by sedatives. There must be no pain, no discomfort and, often, no consciousness. The patient is not allowed to lose interest in staying alive. If a patient gives up and turns his or her face to the wall, cutting off communication with the outside world, the patient may be treated for depression. This idea, that a good death is sudden, is the polar opposite of what was true several hundred years ago (see box).

Dying well in the Middle Ages in Western Europe

In The Hour of Our Death, Phillippe Ariés charts the history of attitudes toward death in Western culture, beginning with the early Middle Ages, where a "good death" was one that gave advance warning. In a good death, one might have a vision or be visited by an apparition, giving one the chance to confess one's sins. An accidental death or murder, unless it occurred during the course of battle in a "just" war, was considered an ugly, vile way to die, and often as a result of wrongdoing on the part of the deceased. Priests often charged a special fee to perform a service for those who had been murdered. Prior to the 1200s or so, death itself was simple for Western Europeans. If one knew one was dying, there was little to do. Dying people simply waited for death, often lying down, crossing their arms across their chests, and facing toward Jerusalem to pray. People took death calmly. At home, the dying person would be surrounded by friends and family who held silent vigil at the bedside. There was no doctor on call, no heroic measures, nothing to do but wait. Ariés describes the attitude toward death as indifferent, resigned, and familiar. Still, the death of a friend or family member was an occasion for much wailing and weeping, as the family moved the body from home to the cemetery.

Finally, Ariés claims that a complete reversal of attitudes is taking place in the U.S. as a result of the work of a few pioneers, including Elizabeth Kübler-Ross and Herman Feifel, who first took it upon themselves to interview the dying. They had the idea that death could be handled with dignity, and dignity first demands that death be recognized. They believed that dying people should have full access to information about their condition and that dying is a proper focus of research. Along with greater curiosity about dying, researchers have also begun to question the unconditional acceptance of medical technology and the prolongation of life beyond the possibility of joy.

In a very recent book, Stephen Jenkinson, an expert on pain management, refers to a managed death as an ordeal. Based on decades of experience in the *death trade*, as he calls it, he writes that what passes for a good death is too often a sedated death accompanied by low-grade terror. In this book, we explore the possibility of dying well—living life until the very end, considering the options, and deciding how one wishes to die, and then making sure that, to the extent it can be accomplished, one's wishes are honored and one's family and friends are at one's side.

References for This Chapter:

Ariés, P. (2008/1982). *The hour of our death: The classic history of Western attitudes toward death over the last one thousand years.* New York, NY: Vintage Books. (Original work published 1982.)

Jenkinson, S. (2015). *Die wise: A manifesto for sanity and soul.* Berkeley, CA: North Atlantic Books.

Kübler-Ross, E. (1969). *On Death and Dying: What the dying have to teach doctors, nurses, clergy, and their own families.* New York, NY: Simon and Schuster.

Light, L. L. (1988). Preserved implicit memory in old age. In M. M. Gruneberg, P. E. Morris, & R. N. Sykes (Eds.). *Practical aspects of memo-*

ry: Current research issues (vol. 2). Hoboken, NJ: Wiley.

Meagher, D. K., & Balk, D. E. (2013). *Handbook of Thanatology.* New York, NY: Routledge.

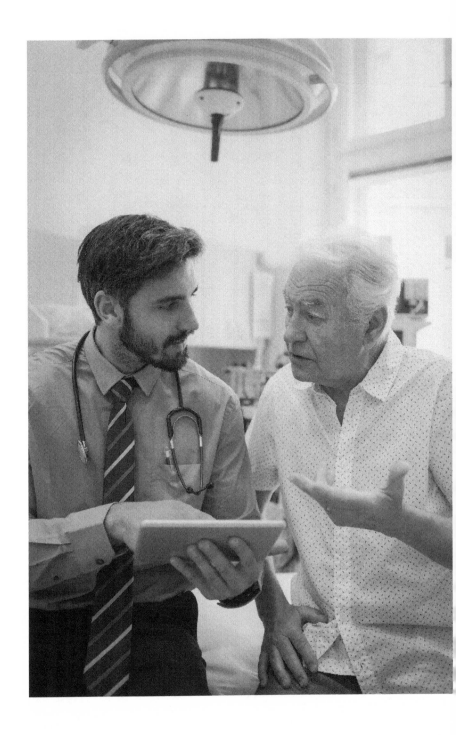

Chapter 2

The Twenty-First Century Model: Personalized and Customized Choices

In 2015, the Institute of Medicine published a report called *Dying in America*, which laid out some of the long-term trends and challenges that are changing the landscape of the death system in the United States. By the year 2030, the report noted, 20% of the population will be over age 65. By 2050, the population over 65 will be twice the size it was in 2012. At the moment, there are 79.4 million baby boomers between the ages of 51 and 71 moving through middle and old age. Very few of them have given any thought to dying or to what are now called *end-of-life* issues. Even among adults over the age of 75, only about a quarter have given any thought to how the end of life should be handled. The number of deaths over the age of 85 is nearly 50 times the number 100 years ago, and many people, as we saw in Chapter 1, have serious, chronic conditions. The report suggested that, in the coming years, the portion of the elderly population with multiple chronic illnesses may rise to as much as two-thirds. The arrival of baby boomers at old age is being called *the Silver Tsunami*.

The Institute's report began with a list of seven major challenges as the U.S. prepares for the arrival of this massive number of elderly citizens.

1. The large number of international immigrants over the past few decades has led to an explosion in cultural diversity and a subsequent focus on the needs and preferences of groups and individuals.

2. The growing divide between the rich and the poor has created greater structural barriers for people who are on the bottom rung of the socioeconomic ladder.

3. Many people are living to a very advanced age—85 or older—so that the number of elderly with mental and cognitive disabilities as well as multiple illnesses is skyrocketing.

4. There are often regional and cultural mismatches between the needs of the elderly and the services that are available.

5. Palliative care (pain and symptom management for chronic diseases) has not kept up with the needs of many chronic and terminal patients.

6. The system often provides perverse incentives to healthcare providers; care delivery is often fragmented, and there is significant time pressure on physicians.

7. The costs of healthcare and end-of-life services are escalating.

Three of every 10 adults are now caregivers for a family member with a serious illness. Most of these people are untrained and stressed emotionally, physically, and financially. People with multiple illnesses often suffer long periods of slow decline punctuated by crises that require repeated hospitalizations. Most caregivers must work to support an ailing family member who is suffering a wide variety of mental and physical problems. Whereas most Americans express a preference for dying at home, just 30% will do so, only a slight improvement from 30 years ago. Another 28% will die in nursing homes, and 70% of those who die after the age of 65 will not be able to make their own decisions in the final days of their lives. Considering the numbers and condition of late-life baby boomers, the Silver Tsunami is likely to overrun the capacity of every facet of the death system, just as boomers have overrun most institutions through which they are moving.

Education and preparation are essential in coping with the baby boomers as they create their final challenge.

It's not just the numbers, though. Baby boomers have wrought deep changes in societal institutions, including marriage, divorce, child-rearing, career development, and the entire spectrum of our educational system. Their financial and social power has fueled changes in how we conceptualize gender roles, religion, love and sex, and work and retirement. They will also, undoubtedly, affect how illness, dying, and bereavement play out in the larger social system.

Very few Americans take time to consider the decisions that attend dying, although most do not want to receive life-extending care, especially if they anticipate cognitive impairment or great pain. The people most likely to plan are the wealthy, because they typically talk about end-of-life care in the process of making a will. Even among the wealthy, communication of relevant sections of a will to a doctor or a hospital requires extra work and is, therefore, spotty at best. Most people don't even have a will, and many don't have a regular healthcare provider who can be informed about end-of-life preferences. Some people are not literate enough to understand the decisions to be made, and others, especially members of marginalized groups, may not believe that the system would work for them no matter how much preparation they undertook.

When people do have regular healthcare, doctors are often reluctant to bring up questions about end of life, especially following the debate about *death panels* that accompanied the Affordable Care Act passed under President Obama. Doctors are concerned that end-of-life discussion will only cause stress, fear, and feelings of hopelessness among people who are fragile. Of course many patients are willing partners in this denial, despite the fact that they want to have a say in what happens to them.

The people who talk about end-of-life decisions in advance are mostly white, educated adults, but only 23% of them put anything in writing, according to the report of the Institute of Medicine. Even those with dependent children do not have wills or advance directives indicating their preferences. The entire 600 pages of the Institute's report is dedicated to making a case for the thoughtful consideration of these preferences to ensure that healthcare "harmonizes with social, psychological, and spiritual support as the end of life approaches," (p. 6). The writers add that end-of-life care should be "person-centered, family-oriented, and evidence-based," (p. 6). This is unlikely if current practices continue.

Advanced Planning

The Institute's report suggested that death education should become a lifelong process, beginning in childhood and continuing through adolescence and adulthood. From talking through the death of a pet in childhood to deciding whether to be an organ donor as a teenager getting a driver's license, there are many teachable moments in early life and young adulthood. Children often do not understand that death is permanent or that it means you can no longer communicate with the living. The Institute's writers were strongly in favor of adults recording and filing *advance directives*, the instructions you leave others about your end-of-life choices.

Advance directives instruct a person's physician about end-of-life decisions, if he or she becomes incapacitated before such decisions need to be implemented. Advance directives typically cover topics such as the use of life-support machinery, including intravenous feeding tubes and machines that ensure continued respiration or heart function. They also cover preferences about resuscitation and the disposition of the body. There is a variety of forms available online that lay out the decisions that need to be made and discuss various options. We will look at some of the forms in some detail in a later chapter.

General guidelines for these decisions can be found in *The Conversation Project*, published by the American Academy of Family Physicians in 2014. This report also points out some of the systemic and cultural problems with the forms available online. For example, in some religious and cultural traditions, the entire family is consulted in these matters. A dying person in these families might feel uncomfortable making choices without involving the group, but physicians tend to prefer to speak to only one person. People who prefer group decisions may not know what to do with the kinds of paperwork that are available and, even if they do, the physician or hospital may ignore their preferences. Moreover, emergency services often don't have any information about a particular patient's preferences until either they arrive at a hospital or the patient's physician appears. More and different forms are required for emergency personnel.

Dying people and their families need strong support in making the decisions they have to make when a crisis arises, and that can be hard to find in a hospital or nursing home. *The Conversation Project* report suggested that nonclinical people be trained to facilitate these discussions. There are a number of organizations around the country that are trying to provide this kind of help. The hospice movement, for example, provides this kind of support, as do some independent organizations such as *Five Wishes.*

At the same time that the Silver Tsunami makes it ever more important to think about one's preferences, the number of these decisions is exploding. Many writers (including the co-authors of this monograph) are calling this the era of the *postmodern death.* In its simplest form, postmodern just refers to what comes after modern. We discussed a "modern" death in Chapter 1, calling it the industrial model, where everything is standardized and commodified. There is a "mainstream" conveyor belt that moves patients from terminal diagnosis through the medical system and finally deposits them in the hands of the funeral industry. Postmodern thinking emphasizes the ways in which reality is what we make of it. Postmodernist thinkers value choice, individuality, and differences. What this means for the dying is that you can pretty much plan your own journey any way you like. There is no one best way to handle dying. It's an individual matter.

You can tell your physician that you want to know every last detail of your diagnosis and prognosis, or you can tell your physician that you don't want to talk about anything but treatment options. You can decide to do something about your condition, do nothing about it, or anything in between. You can die at home in a lounge chair in the backyard, or in an intensive care unit with healthcare providers that will do everything they can to save you. You can be buried in the ground, cremated and placed in a niche at Forest Lawn, or have your ashes scattered. You can be buried at sea. You can plan an elaborate funeral or a simple memorial service or ask that people do nothing.

How on earth do we choose among all the options? There is some evidence about what works and what doesn't work, of course, but we are just beginning to understand the implications of these new possibilities. Some people are afraid to plan for their own death because they fear it will make them more anxious or even hasten their death. There is no evidence that shows this to be the case, and what evidence we do have demonstrates that planning alleviates the suffering of survivors. It relieves them of the burden of decision making and, in particular, from worrying about whether they have made the right decision. Planning eliminates conflict between family members and the need to guess what the dying person would want.

The Institute of Medicine also encourages doctors and patients to share decision making. Doctors need to understand the patient's perspective and emotional state and to be able to take stock of the patient's social context. Patients and doctors benefit from developing shared understandings about treatment goals and outcomes. Doctors and patients need to "hope for the best and prepare for the worst," managing symptoms, building support, and maintaining dignity along the way. The report of *The Conversation Project* noted that poor quality conversations, especially during a crisis, and inadequate training of hospital personnel and healthcare agents impair the ability of families to receive the strong support they need in making the decisions they have to make. The report recommended that nonclinical people be trained to facilitate these discussions. There are many organizations around the country that are trying to do just that. Hospices, which we will discuss in a moment, often provide this kind of support.

The Hospice Movement

The word *hospice* has the same root as the word *hospitality*. In the Middle Ages, a hospice was a place where weary sojourners might find rest along the road. The idea of a hospice as a sanctuary for the dying was first promulgated by Cecily Saunders in London during the late 1960s. She believed that patients should be maintained free of pain and that social and emotional impoverishment should be kept to a minimum. She emphasized providing support for competent behavior among patients and giving them the opportunity to resolve conflicts and fulfill realistic wishes. She also acknowledged that patients must be able to seek or relinquish relationships and control when they do so.

Cecily Saunders wanted to free patients not only from the pain itself but also from the fear of pain. In the hospitals of the time, for example, pain medication was typically given every two to four hours when patients' pain reached a point where they asked for medication. Saunders felt that patients should be given pain medication regularly, every 2 to 4 hours, before they have to ask for it. She recommended a combination of morphine, cocaine, and gin, known as a Brompton's Cocktail, which left the patient both alert and pain free.

Saunders also argued that the role of staff in a hospice is not to *do* anything for the patient, but to *be* with the patient. She was adamant that patients not be treated as objects, even when unconscious. She wanted to place more emphasis on personal needs and appearance than medical tests and procedures. She also hoped to provide support for a family that wanted to keep a patient at home.

Following Saunders's lead, the hospice movement in the United States is dedicated to making the shift from delaying death to improving what remains of life. The National Hospice and Palliative Care Organization (NHPCO) offers this definition of hospice:

> Hospice provides support and care for persons in the last
> phases of an incurable disease so that they may live as ful-
> ly and as comfortably as possible. Hospice recognizes that
> the dying process is part of the normal process of living
> and focuses on enhancing the quality of remaining life.
> (NHPCO, 2000, p. II)

The hospice movement would not be possible, however, without *palliative care*. On its webpage, the Mayo Clinic defines palliative care as:

...specialized medical care that focuses on providing patients relief from pain and other symptoms of a serious illness, no matter the diagnosis or stage of disease. Palliative-care teams aim to improve the quality of life for both patients and their families. This form of care is offered alongside curative or other treatments that [patients] may receive.

The NHPCO points out that palliative care should be patient- and family-centered and address the physical, psychological, social, and spiritual needs of the patient. It should also facilitate patient autonomy, access to information, and choice.

Hospices usually provide or coordinate palliative care, which can be delivered in a variety of ways. It may be administered in a standalone facility, such as Serenity House in Santa Barbara, California (see box), or housed in a hospital, a nursing home, or an assisted-care facility. Most frequently, a hospice in the United States is a set of special services integrated into a hospital setting. There may be a hospice or a palliative-care ward in which the usual rules and regulations are relaxed, allowing family and friends, including children, to stay beyond normal visiting hours. Sometimes, hospice is not a place at all, but an organization that provides support to families wishing to keep a dying patient at home.

Serenity House

Serenity House is an 18-bed inpatient hospice house that provides care for hospice patients whose needs cannot be met at home. Hidden on a hillside among Santa Barbara's majestic coastal oaks, it's a place where our patients are cared for in a serene and homelike setting. Each private room allows patients to be surrounded by loved ones throughout their time with us. Serenity House provides round-the-clock medical care from a team of specially trained doctors, a nurse practitioner, nurses, social workers, spiritual counselors, hospice aides, and volunteers that support emotional, spiritual, and practical concerns. Information gathered from http://www.vnhcsb.org/serenity-house/ on August 24, 2017.

Serenity House in Santa Barbara, CA

Hospice organizations help families provide a humane, caring environment for the dying patient and ease the guilt the family may feel about not pursuing extremely expensive, and often unwanted, hospital care. Remember, if patients refuse treatment in the hospital, they must be moved to a nursing home or other such facility or go home. Hospices also provide medical support for palliative care at home and volunteer services that support families by offering simple household services such as running errands. Volunteer hospices, such as the one described below, are also available. Volunteers provide companionship for patients and respite for caregivers. A volunteer hospice provides services, but does not offer housing. The Hospice of Santa Barbara works with both the local hospital and Serenity House to support patients who choose to stay at home as long as possible.

The *Handbook of Thanatology* notes that the hospice movement is one of the most successful grassroots movements of the last quarter of the twentieth century. This movement has led us to question how well the medical system generally meets the needs of those who are dying. There are problems, of course, associated with every kind of end-of-life care. Some researchers argue that when hospice is integrated into the hospital setting, a strong, vocal advocate is required to support it, given that hospitals do not ordinarily adopt the idea that the patient knows best.

The Hospice of Santa Barbara

Hospice of Santa Barbara, Inc., provides compassionate care and support to those impacted with serious illness and the bereaved. It is the second oldest hospice program in the United States. Through its Patient Care Services program, individuals can receive comprehensive care from the time they are diagnosed and move interchangeably among programs depending on what services they need at that moment. Traditional medical hospice models require a six-month or less prognosis and the discontinuation of curative treatments to receive service. The Patient Care Services program serves the newly diagnosed or those pursuing their preferred treatment choices. Hospice of Santa Barbara's counselors also offer free, confidential, professional counseling to anyone grieving the death of a loved or coping with a life-threatening illness. Bereavement services include individual counseling, support groups, art workshops, therapeutic poetry, and holiday workshops for every age group. www.hospiceofsantabarbara.org

The Hospice of Santa Barbara

On the other hand, when hospice services are provided in the home, it can get expensive and burdensome for the family. Proper care may require house calls by physicians, nurses, healthcare aides, and social workers. Without adequate support, families can become highly stressed and physically exhausted. Most American hospices are funded by Medicare and only admit patients with terminal illnesses carrying a prognosis of six months or less. Patients must give up curative treatment in order to receive the hospice benefits provided by Medicare, but there is much disagreement about what "curative" treatment is and is not. Many treatments are designed to prolong life (sometimes for months or even years), but are not curative. Many patients who are not willing to give up treatment delay hospice admission unnecessarily, not aware that it's actually the hospice provider who determines what is and what isn't considered to be curative.

Although Medicare will fund up to six months of hospice care and sometimes more, few patients receive this much care. As we have noted, doctors often fight death harder than patients do, and they may be reluctant to refer patients to a hospice. Most patients will only use a few weeks of hospice care at the end of their lives. In 2012, for example, NPHCO reported that, despite the fact that nearly half of all deaths in the United States occurred in a hospice, over 35% of these patients receive care for less than seven days. Furthermore, when people do not have Medicare or other insurance, they must pay for their own care or must rely on funds that are raised by hospice providers. A few hospices provide social and emotional support for free, like Hospice of Santa Barbara, which is supported by private donations and grants. The National Palliative and Hospice Care Organization can be found at: https://www.nhpco.org/.

Baby boomers are the first generation to take full advantage of hospice services both for themselves and for their elderly parents. Many writers believe that baby boomers are already changing the death system, just as they have changed all of the institutions they have touched. Boomers are opening up the options around death and dying and have led a trend toward more personalization. Combined with the options that have been advanced in response to an increasingly diverse society, there is great pressure on all end-of-life services to be more flexible and individualized.

Boomers are more willing to talk about death than earlier generations. They have created new venues where the topic can be addressed, such as death cafés and death-themed dinners. Books and guides have proliferated, including bestsellers such as *Being Mortal,* by Atul Gwande, a physician who advocates for medical practices that enhance living rather than prolong dying, and a series of books by Kűbler-Ross on dying, grieving, and even life after death.

Changes in American demographics are also impacting the funeral industry in myriad ways. For example, more boomers prefer to be cremated and are aware that there are many ways to deal with the ashes. Ashes can be bundled up in a fountain or birdbath in the garden or planted at the root of a tree. They can be put in orbit for years or shot to the moon. They can be scattered in multiple places, sealed into a locket, or become part of an artificial reef.

The National Association of Funeral Directors informs us that contemporary funerals can incorporate not only a person's religious tradition, but also their hobbies, their interests, and their unique personal attributes. Was your uncle an avid camper? You can build a camp site as a venue for the memorial service. Did he belong to a band? The remaining crew can play his favorite tunes at the funeral. Did he enjoy reenacting the Revolutionary war? He can be buried in his uniform and have his face printed on a personalized postage stamp. The National Association of Funeral Directors can be contacted by visiting http://www.nfda.org/.

Death and the Baby Boom

Boomers are also the first generation that has tried to care, en masse, for elderly parents who have multiple chronic and terminal illnesses. The parents of the boomer generation have lived longer than any earlier generation and, because of that longevity, have higher rates of Alzheimer's disease, chronic arthritis, incontinence, and diabetes than previous generations. Many writers believe that the boomers are going to be the first generation to question whether they want to get an extra decade of life by living in a nursing home and going in and out of the hospital. In 2013, *Time* magazine reported that we are seeing the emergence of aid-in-dying as the next civil rights movement. Several states, including Vermont, Oregon, Washington, Montana, and California, have passed laws legalizing assisted dying. Campaigns are underway in half-a-dozen more states.

Over the next 20 years, the American funeral industry is expected to show a $7 million surge in profits. Twenty years from now, the baby boomers will be rapidly dying off. Ten thousand baby boomers a day retire and begin receiving Medicare and Social Security benefits, as reported by the Social Security Administration in 2012. Does this mean that soon 10,000 baby boomers will die every day for the next 20 years? How will that impact culture in the U.S. and in the other countries that reported increased birth rates after World War II? There are already heated debates about how retirement will affect the economy and the leadership of organizations. The implications for housing and healthcare and for the burden on families will be enormous. The demand for end-of-life services, like the demand for elementary schools in the sixties, college placement in the seventies, and childcare in the eighties, will skyrocket.

Other aging countries, such as Japan, are already facing shortages of funeral services. Like the boomers, Japanese prefer cremation, yet crematoriums in Japan are so backed up that families are waiting for several days before the body can be cremated. In the meantime, a whole new industry is growing up around how to care for the body after the person has died and before the body can be dispatched. There are entire hotels (*itai hoteru* or corpse hotels) devoted to caring for the remains and offering the family an opportunity to perform the traditional rituals.

The rest of this book is devoted to exploring all of the challenges and possibilities inherent in this kind of change. We began, simply, by asking how exactly death is defined. In Chapter 3, we cover biological, psychological, and social death.

References for This Chapter:

Byock, I. (2012). *The best care possible.* New York, NY: Avery/Penguin Books.

Leland, J. (2018). The Positive Death Movement comes to Life. *New York Times,* June 22. Retrieved from www.nytimes.com June 24, 2018.

Ostaseski, F. (2017). *The five invitations: Discovering what death can teach us about living fully.* New York, NY: Flatiron Books.

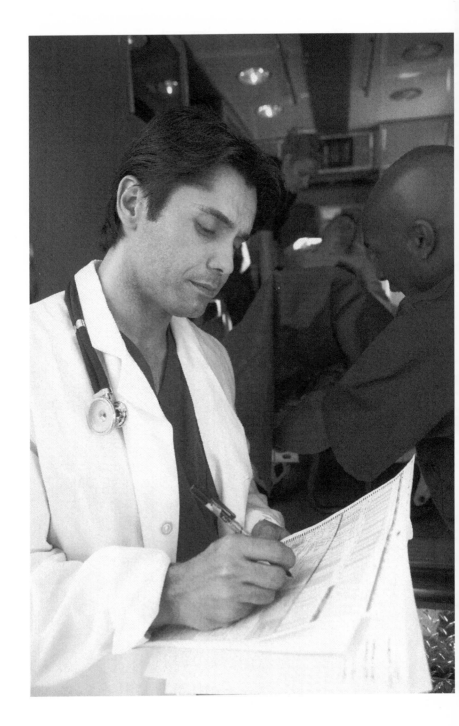

Chapter 3

The evolving definition of death: What we know now

You'd think it would be simple to say whether or not someone is dead, but it hasn't ever been, really. There are many accounts of people who were thought to be dead who turned out later to be alive. In fact, this happened often enough over the centuries that coffins were sometimes designed with bells that could be rung or flags that could be raised from the inside. Today, technology lets us bring people back from the dead with machines that restart your heart and re-inflate your lungs. Death is generally defined as the cessation of all the biological, psychological, and social processes that attend the life of a person, but each of these components can occur without the other two and, in fact, all three rarely happen together.

For centuries, a person was considered dead when a heartbeat could no longer be detected and breathing stopped. Today, we can keep people alive by this definition for weeks, months, and even years, raising numerous questions. For example, criminal law requires that the victim be dead if someone is to be accused of murder. There are other areas of law about wrongful death and the rights and duties of survivors that depend upon how death is defined.

In 1981, a presidential commission issued the Uniform Determination of Death Act, which states that a dead person is someone who has suffered either irreversible cessation of circulatory and respiratory function OR irreversible cessation of all functions of the entire brain. These criteria have been accepted by the American Medical Association and the American

Bar Association. By this definition, however, a person might still be alive as long as brain stem reflexes can be detected, even if the person no longer is capable of consciousness or social interaction.

The presidential commission acknowledged the traditional idea that heart function and respiration are to be considered, but essentially endorsed the Harvard Criteria of Total Brain Death shown below. No person meeting these criteria has ever regained any brain function. No reasonable person would argue that someone who meets all of the Harvard Criteria is alive, yet there is still controversy about whether someone who does not meet all of the criteria, but shows no sign of higher brain function, is still alive. The commission eventually adopted the Harvard Criteria because they found it too difficult to agree on a definition of personhood or consciousness.

A Summary of the Harvard Criteria of Death

1. Unreceptivity and unresponsivity. The individual is totally unaware of externally applied stimuli and inner need and is completely unresponsive.

2. No movements or breathing. Observation of at least one hour reveals no spontaneous muscular movements, spontaneous respiration, nor response to stimuli such as pain, touch, sound, or light. Total absence of respiration after the patient is on a mechanical respirator maybe determined by turning off the respirator for three minutes and observing whether there is any effort on the part of the patient to breathe spontaneously.

3. No reflexes: The pupils of the eyes are fixed and dilated and do not respond to intense light. Ocular movements, in response to head turning or irrigating the ears with ice water, and all blinking movements are absent. There is no swallowing, yawning, or vocalization and no postural activity. There are no tendon reflexes or planar response, and the application of noxious stimuli has no effect.

4. *Flat electroencephalogram.* Given that the EEG electrodes are properly applied, the apparatus is functioning properly, and the personnel in charge are competent, a flat EEG is of "great confirmatory value," if hypothermia (temperature below 90 degrees Fahrenheit) or the use of central nervous system depressants, such as barbiturates, are excluded.

5. All of the above tests shall be repeated at least twenty-four hours later with no change.

SOURCE: Based on "A definition of Irreversible Coma." (1968)

The Uniform Death Act does not specify what instruments or technologies must be used to measure any of these functions. In the end, we have to rely on the judgment of a physician. When the physician decides that a person is dead, all attempts to sustain that person's life cease, so even if the person is alive in some sense, he or she will soon be dead. Death is both a medical decision and a legal status. When a person dies, none of the rights and privileges of the living still apply and the body becomes a kind of property, since it is now necessary for someone to take possession of it and make decisions about organ donation, autopsy, and what to do with the remains.

Here is where things get complicated. The law, the Uniform Anatomical Gift Act, which has been adopted by most states in the U.S., expressly grants to the next of kin the right to make decisions about organ donation. Consent of the next of kin, however, is not required if the deceased made an organ donation before dying, and the donation of one organ does not mean that more organs cannot be donated after death. A person can become a donor by signing a document or by allowing a document to be signed by someone else in the presence of two witnesses. A person can also become a donor by designation on a driver's license, and that designation is still valid even if the license is revoked or suspended. If the deceased has expressed the desire to be a donor, no one can revoke it; and if the deceased has refused to be a donor, no one can revoke that either.

Despite rumors to the contrary, a family does not have to decide to "pull the plug" to make an organ donation. Once the person is declared dead by a physician, life support is terminated. Families can decide to take a person off of life support when the heart stops beating on its own even when some signs of brain stem function remain. If the organs are to be transplanted, they must be maintained in good condition by machines. Families are often confused when this happens. They haven't digested the fact that the patient has been pronounced dead. When a person's heart stops on the operating table, decisions have to be made quickly and family members may feel that they did not get enough information about brain death or that they didn't consent to this particular situation, when, in fact, they had. Families need time to process the information they receive, and hospital staff need to take care about how the information is shared and to be aware of the family's emotional needs.

For more information about approaches to organ preservation, see https://www.ncbi.nim.nih.gov/pmc/articles/PMC3088753/

Psychological and Social Death

Although we know hearts can keep beating and lungs can still fill with air long after the person we know is gone, there is no definition for psychological death. The president's commission that gave us a definition of biological death was stumped when it tried to define personhood. For families struggling with a family member who has Alzheimer's disease or is in a coma, this question is front and center. Some writers in the field have argued that it is immoral to treat a body that is essentially without personhood as though it were a person. Some believe that once higher function is no longer possible, the body should not be maintained. One of the founders of the field of thanatology, Robert Kastenbaum, suggested that we define psychological death in terms of whether the person is dead to him or herself, but that only raises the question of what it means to be dead to oneself and how we would know it.

Sometimes these issues become public sensations, as in the case of Karen Quinlin, who collapsed at a party after taking Valium washed down with alcohol. The hospital was able to prevent her biological death, but she suffered profound brain damage and was then maintained in a vegetative state. After a long legal battle, the family won the right to remove her from life support machinery, but she continued to live in a coma for almost 10 years after that. The case was hotly debated in the media, even though the court decided that this is what Karen Quinlan herself would have wanted. In a similar case, after months of legal battles, the parents won the right to withdraw a feeding tube from their daughter, Nancy Cruz, who was left in a vegetative state after an automobile accident in 1981. Her parents took the case to court in 1990. She died a month later.

Biological death is only one aspect of the problem. There is also psychological and social death, which are deeply intertwined. When a person can no longer interact with others, the behavior of others begins to change. The survivors begin to talk about someone who is psychologically dead as though the person were biologically dead. Survivors no longer make eye contact and cease trying to have a conversation with the dying person. They stop touching the person and begin to make decisions about the person's health care without even attempting consultation.

How does the family make a decision to end the use of life support? This is where it becomes critical to know what the person who is dying would have wanted. Both the Quinlan and Cruz cases were resolved by the parents bringing evidence showing that Karen and Nancy would have wanted their parents to let them go. In the case of Nancy Cruz, the U.S. Supreme Court had to decide the case when it was brought on appeal from the state of Missouri. These cases make it clear how important it is that people of all ages who are capable of discussing death and dying express their wishes. As difficult as it is to talk to a teenager or young adult about dying, it's important to try. Not understanding what someone would have wanted can cause social, psychological, and financial distress, as well as legal problems.

In this society, complete biological and psychological death usually occur together, with social death following swiftly on their heels. There are some places in the world, however, where social death can precede psychological death. In tribal life, a person may be shunned for breaking social taboos. Even in contemporary society, people can experience a partial social death whenever they are excluded from an important aspect of their social network. Here again, social death is inextricably intertwined with psychological death. When you lose an important relationship, you lose the part of yourself that existed in relationship to that person. An example of social and psychological death that almost all of us experience occurs when our parents die. Middle-aged and older people speak of being orphaned when their parents die. We feel the loss of the part of ourselves that was a child. Extreme examples occur in our society when people leaving a cult or religious community are shunned.

There is also evidence that biological death can precede psychological death. Near-death may not convince a scientist that there is life after death, but it does make it clear that biological death and psychological death can occur independently. We will discuss these experiences in some depth at the end of this book, as they evoke all kinds of questions about what we believe about death and how we should treat the dead.

For most of us, biological, psychological, and social death will occur at pretty much the same time. Through funerals, memorials, and bereavements—which can last for days, weeks, or years—survivors cease looking for, talking to and, eventually, thinking of the dead. The death of one person has many social consequences. Relationships are lost. When a spouse dies, the couple no longer exists. When a father dies, the family is ruptured. When a friend dies, the social networks of other people are diminished. At work, a position is vacated; at church, a member is lost. For the bereaved, a social death demands the reorganization of their relationships. How each survivor handles the loss of this relationship will depend upon the meaning death has for them, and part of that meaning depends upon how and why someone died.

Causes of Death

In this chapter, we talk about dying of natural causes across the lifespan. The impact of an unexpected death, whether due to accident, suicide, or homicide, requires special attention and thus occupies a later chapter. The leading causes of death are different for people of different ages. Most infants die of conditions associated with their birth or from sudden infant death syndrome. Accidents, cancer, and congenital problems account for most deaths of children under 10. Homicide and suicide become more common in late childhood and early adolescence. Among adults, nearly a quarter of all deaths occur due to heart disease and another quarter due to cancer. Chronic respiratory and cardiovascular problems (like aneurysms) round out the top four causes. Accidents are the fifth most frequent cause of death in adulthood. Alzheimer's, diabetes, and kidney disease each account for about 2% of all deaths and suicide another 1.6%. Most importantly, two-thirds of people over 65 have multiple chronic diseases. People who have multiple chronic conditions account for about two-thirds of all Medicare payments.

Common chronic conditions in older people include high blood pressure, high cholesterol, arthritis, depression, osteoporosis, and asthma. As the baby boomers age over the next 20 years, it is expected that the number of people with cancer and heart disease will grow dramatically. By the year 2030, a 45% increase is expected in the number of cancer cases. Alzheimer's is expected to jump from the current 5.5 million people to 8.7 million. Between now and 2032, the numbers of Americans who need long-term care will more than double, to include some 27 million individuals.

In the late nineties, the Institute of Medicine released a report called *Approaching Death: Improving care at the end of life* (1997). The report outlines three common paths or trajectories that people experience near the end of life. Some people die from an unexpected cause, such as an auto-mobile accident or a stroke. Others experience a steady decline associat-ed with a progressive disease that has a terminal phase, such as cancer. A third trajectory includes people with chronic diseases such as lung disease or chronic heart failure, which progress through a steady decline, with peri-odic crises and, eventually, a sudden death.

Most often children die either from a sudden death, such as sudden infant death syndrome, or a disease that fluctuates as it declines, such as heart failure. Dying children often experience constant medical fragility as, for example, when they have neurological diseases. Most adolescents die from either cancer or a sudden death, such as an accident. Many physical, social, and cultural variables affect the experience of people who are dying with chronic diseases, but as people move toward the end of life, most will report certain common symptoms.

Chronic diseases in the last few months of life are characterized by pain, poor appetite, weakness, and fatigue. Shortness of breath, nausea, and vomiting often occur, along with difficulty in swallowing and bowel problems. All kinds of minor irritations arise, including dry mouth, dental problems, and sores. Itching, swelling, dryness, and sensitivity to touch are frequent complaints. There are also psychological issues such as confusion, anxiety, and depression. These symptoms are experienced by anyone dying of a chronic disease, regardless of age. The box offers a description of what it is like to cope with multiple chronic diseases.

Living with Multiple Chronic Diseases

Cindy, a 78-year-old retired nurse, has undergone 10 different surgical procedures over the last 16 years. Her spine has been fused at two difference places, and she has had a disc removed in her lumbar spine, had a total hip replacement, broke her pelvis twice, and has broken her tibia. She has had two cancerous tumors removed from her mouth and has had a pacemaker installed. She suffers from chronic obstructive pulmonary disease (COPD) as well as rheumatoid arthritis, high blood pressure, and gastroesophageal reflux disease (GERD).

Cindy still thinks clearly, communicates well, and continues to live alone in her own two-story home. She walks with a walker and has figured out how to climb the stairs to her bedroom. She organizes and maintains a network of caregivers that do her shopping and light chores around the house, and take her to doctor appointments and to have her nails done occasionally. Her meals are delivered by Meals on Wheels. She has a regular housekeeper, a gardener, and a hairdresser who comes to the house. She has completed and filed a power of attorney and medical directives and has planned and prepaid for her funeral arrangements and burial.

Despite it all, she has a great sense of humor and continues to love the adventures life brings. She is my hero. I am her hospice volunteer. *Jane, a hospice volunteer in Santa Barbara.*

People suffering from multiple chronic conditions must also cope with the interactions of these conditions. A treatment that is effective in treating osteoporosis, for example, may cause stomach problems. Cancer treatment often aggravates heart and neurological conditions. Alzheimer's makes almost everything more difficult because patients cannot communicate effectively with caregivers or participate in and monitor their own care.

This astounding array of conditions and symptoms often requires an equally astounding array of caretakers, including various kinds of nurses, from nursing assistants to those registered nurses who specialize in advanced diseases. Physical therapists and rehabilitation specialists, nutritionists, social workers, and pharmacists may be involved, along with family caregivers and hospice volunteers. At the Seattle Cancer Care Alliance, for example, one of the authors, who was diagnosed with stage 3 colon cancer, was assigned a team that included an oncologist, a physician's assistant, a pharmacist, a social worker, a phlebotomist, a nutritionist, a nurse educator, and two nurses who supervised her chemotherapy. Aside from her mainstream healthcare providers, she also engaged an acupuncturist, a naturopath, and a hairdresser who specialized in "cancer hair." The Seattle Cancer Care Alliance also offered the opportunity to see a licensed psychotherapist or a psychiatrist if she felt the need for it.

With all of this going on, it seems clear that coordination of care becomes critical. Often this role is played by the patient's primary care physician, who might be a family physician, an internist, a geriatrician, or a nurse practitioner or physician's assistant. But the dying patient often has so many specialty caregivers that coordination among them is next to impossible. There is good evidence, all the same, that a coordinator can play an important role in the patient's experience of care, especially in meeting the patient's needs for communication and emotional support. One recent study reported that advanced lung cancer patients experienced 25% fewer admissions to critical care units if they were seen by their primary care provider during their final hospitalization.

Coordination of Care

Another important problem arising from multiple chronic conditions is that people near the end of life often experience numerous relocations that affect their health and well-being. People may be admitted to the hospital from home on numerous occasions. Before they do go home again, they may move to a nursing home or rehabilitation facility. Once discharged, they may need to move from independent living to assisted care, from intensive care to a palliative care unit if they refuse treatment, or from home to a hospice when the family can no longer provide the appropriate level of care.

Many times poorly managed transitions result in readmissions to the hospital. One large study, reviewed in the 2015 report of the Institute of Medicine, showed that patients who were enrolled in a program that assigned a nurse to assess the patient's needs at the time of discharge were not only readmitted to the hospital less frequently, they also stayed in the hospital for shorter periods of time when they were readmitted. Another study demonstrated that the use of a "transition coach," who worked with caregivers during relocation, produced better outcomes. At the Seattle Cancer Care Alliance, a nurse educator is given the task of ensuring that patients and caregivers know whom to contact, understand the management of medication, and are aware of the red flags that might indicate significant problems.

We all know how difficult it is to move. One of the authors once wrote a piece entitled "Residential Moving Psychosis" to describe the confusion and disorientation associated with a perfectly normal move undertaken by reasonably healthy, middle-aged people. For a person with multiple chronic conditions, especially if one of those conditions is Alzheimer's disease or dementia, a simple move from independent living to the hospital and then to an assisted care unit or a nursing home can be a nightmare. Families are called upon to sort through the patient's belongings, packing up what can be carried to a nursing home or assisted care unit, moving whatever furniture is permitted in the new setting, and assisting in all kinds of decision making that the patient may be unable or unwilling to do.

Patients often lose authority over their own lives during such transitions. They may not be consulted about what to keep, what to throw away, where to put things, whether they can make their own choices about what they eat, or where they can go. Anger and depression arise along with confusion and disorientation, making it more difficult to engage in comforting social interactions, to accept care, and to tolerate inordinate delays. Such complexity can make it very difficult to ensure that patients get the care they need. "I just want to go home" is a common response of patients to all this change.

The World Health Organization (WHO) calls chronic diseases "noncommunicable" and points out that prevention is the best way to address them. In a series of reports, they recently estimated that cardiovascular diseases, cancers, chronic respiratory diseases, and diabetes account for 60% of all deaths globally and that 80% of heart disease, stroke, and type 2 diabetes, as well as a third of all cancers, could be prevented by changes in lifestyle. These diseases are all linked to physical inactivity, an unhealthy diet, and the use of tobacco and alcohol. Across the globe, WHO advocates for work at both the international and national levels to integrate the prevention and control of such diseases into governmental policies. There is also a good argument to be made here for the use of non-allopathic medicine. Naturopathy, acupuncture, Chinese medicine, and nutrition can make a difference in impeding the progress of chronic illness and improving the patient's comfort. Chapter 8 presents a point of view drawn from work on nutrition and chronic disease.

For the foreseeable future we are going to be coping as individuals, as families, and as a nation with the fallout of chronic diseases, including their impact on every system involved in end-of-life services. One of the most important things we can do to ensure that the healthcare system remains functional is to face the facts head on and have the difficult conversations that are required to prepare.

References for This Chapter:

Field, M. J., Cassel, C. K. (Eds). (1997). *Approaching death: Improving care at the end of life.* Washington, DC: National Academies Press. https://www.ncbi.nlm.nih.gov/books/NBK233601

World Health Organization (2013). 2008–2013 Action Plan for the Global Strategy for the Prevention and Control of Noncommunicable Diseases: prevent and control cardiovascular diseases, cancers, chronic respiratory diseases and diabetes. WHO Document Production Services, Geneva, Switzerland.

PART TWO

Let's talk about living and dying

CHAPTER 4

BRINGING IT UP: THE CONVERSATION

This chapter is about both how to start a conversation about the end of life when there is no crisis and how to have that conversation if and when you learn you have a mortal illness. The same conversation might take place before or after you find out you are dying. The best time to have it is before you need to, though that, in some ways, is harder. There doesn't seem to be any rush before the need arises, so the discussion is easily put off. As the writers of *The Conversation Project* put it, "It's always too early until it's too late" (see https://www.aafp.org/patient-care/inform/conversation-project.html).

Knowing what the issues are is a good place to begin. If you have children, you may have already started this conversation by discussing whom you would want to raise your children if something happens to you. Most young couples have this conversation with each other, as well as the people they hope to appoint as guardians. Guardianship can open a door to a more extended discussion of what would happen if one member of the couple—or both—is incapacitated because of an accident or an unexpected health crisis.

Ordinarily, spouses depend upon each other to speak for them if they are unable to speak for themselves, but you can designate anyone you like to assume this role. The research shows that spouses are usually fairly accurate in thinking through what the other member of the couple would want, although wives are better at it than husbands. Older, unmarried people and widows usually choose an adult child if they have one. People without close family choose a friend.

Steven's Advice

There are seemingly endless ways of avoiding the simple fact that we won't live forever. Preparing for future medical decisions is important, but something that can be difficult for many people to do. We're likely to put off thinking about complex and sensitive issues. We make the mistake of believing there'll be a better time later. Somehow it always seems to feel too soon, until it's too late.

The good news is we have the right to make our own healthcare decisions. The bad news is we rarely discuss those decisions with others ahead of time. An advance directive is a legal form that outlines the types of medical care we'd like to receive if we are very sick or injured and unable to communicate, as well as the treatment we would not like to receive. Advance care planning is more complex than a simple DNR order. If people misunderstand and think that such planning is all about the documents, it sounds quite narrow. But end-of-life planning is really all about defining meaning in life and deepening relationships, and empowerment through choices and informed decision making.

I have a healthcare directive, not because I have a serious illness, but because I have a family. For me end-of-life decision making is about doing what is important to you, whatever that may mean to you. And saying what we need to say now, and not waiting until it's too late. Steven, a university instructor in death education

Choosing a Healthcare Agent

Fully 90% of the people surveyed for *The Conversation Project* thought it was important to discuss their end-of-life preferences, yet only 30% reported that they had actually talked to their family about their preferences. An unexpected death or terminal diagnosis of a friend or acquaintance can provide a starting point for this discussion, as well as articles about end-of-life choices or popular books, such as *Tuesdays with Morrie*. Of course, you can share this book as a way to begin. Even people who are quite anxious about having the conversation can be convinced by stories about friends who had unexpectedly found themselves in a life-threatening situation. You may have to bring up the subject several times. Don't push, but do persist.

It is particularly important to have a wide-ranging conversation with the person you choose to make end-of-life decisions for you, known as your *healthcare agent*. Healthcare agents should know you well, and they must be at least 18 years of age and willing to discuss the choices that have to be made. A healthcare agent should be a person who can stand up for your wishes and know the differences between his or her feelings and yours. It should be someone who can work with the people who are providing care for you and with the friends and family members who might question your decisions. An agent needs to have the ability to listen to you, to your care providers, and to those who care about you—no small requirement. The person you select must also be able to challenge physicians and other healthcare providers if they try to ignore or override your decisions.

Even when there is a healthcare agent and the patient has made it clear that they don't want to be resuscitated or to receive life-extending treatments, those orders may be ignored, especially by emergency personnel or in a fast-breaking crisis. Physicians tend to default to the safer position of trying to save a person's life when there is no active intervention by the patient or the healthcare agent. In one study, nearly three-quarters of physicians interviewed said they would not honor a patient's do-not-resuscitate order or would hesitate to do so in an emergency.

The research shows that creating a plan for the care you'll need at the end of your life in advance has several emotional, social, and psychological benefits. It relieves stress for family members who might otherwise feel conflicted about what to do. It gives the patient a sense of control and makes it easier to communicate about other things. Among children and adolescent patients, it promotes more positive attitudes. Among the elderly, family members suffer less anxiety and depression after the death of a loved one if they believe they understood the patient's wishes.

For reasons such as these, experts recommend a comprehensive approach to end-of-life care called *advance care planning*, which includes a broad discussion of preferences and values that are set down in writing or in a video statement. A *durable power of attorney*, a legal form that names the healthcare agent, is the cornerstone of advance care planning. You should also consider creating medical orders that bind doctors and emergency personnel to carry out your wishes. Both of these forms are discussed in Chapter 7 on legal matters, but suffice it to say here that effective planning depends on your knowing what you want and talking to your healthcare agent about it.

Advance Directives

Here are a few of the questions you should consider with your agent. If you are in a situation where you can't make choices for yourself and there's no expectation that you'll recover from your mental or physical disabilities to live a reasonably normal life, do you want to be resuscitated if your heart stops? Do you want to be kept on life-maintaining machines if there is little or no chance you can recover your physical or mental health? Do you want to be kept alive by feeding and hydration if you are in a vegetative state? Answering these questions is hard in the moment, but it can save everyone a lot of grief in the long run. These preferences are usually laid out in advance directives to physicians. Let's consider a specific example.

Each state has its own legal forms for advance directives that can be downloaded or obtained from physicians and hospitals. In the State of California, the form allows you to name a person to make decisions for you and to list other people in the order you would choose if your first choice is unable or unwilling to be present. The California form states that you have the right to consent to or refuse any care, treatment, service, or procedure to maintain, diagnose, or otherwise affect a physical or mental condition. It also allows you to state your preferences about organ donation, the use of autopsy, and the disposition of remains.

The first part of the form, called the *Power of Attorney for Healthcare*, is where you designate individuals who can serve as healthcare agents. In the second part of the form, you describe your healthcare preferences, including whether you want your life to be prolonged if you (a) have an incurable and irreversible condition that will result in your death; (b) become unconscious with no hope of regaining consciousness; or (c) are being considered for interventions where the "risks and burdens of treatment would outweigh the expected benefits." In this section of the form, you can also request treatment that will alleviate pain or discomfort even if it hastens your death. The form provides several places for you to customize your directives.

Customizing the form is probably a good idea. Most of us are well aware that machines can keep hearts beating and lungs breathing long after we are psychologically gone, but there is a wide array of other life-support systems you may want to mention in the conversations you have with your agent and your family. Unless you discuss these things, most doctors are likely to follow routine protocols for prolonging life.

For most people, the hardest decisions are the ones that involve feeding and hydration. When families withdraw a feeding tube or intravenous hydration, it can be emotionally agonizing. There is something profoundly disturbing about refusing someone you love food and water. It is critical, therefore, to address these issues for them in advance. The box describes the experience that one of the authors had making such a decision without specific orders from her dying mother. Other treatments that are considered life sustaining include renal dialysis, chemotherapy, the installation of pacemakers, and the use of antibiotics. If you are going to die in a short time anyway, do you want these kinds of treatments?

Judy's Story

My mother, Elaine, had a DNR (Do Not Resuscitate) form on file at the hospital. She had also made clear that she did not want to receive any further treatment or go to the hospital again. She had been living with end-stage emphysema for 10 years; she was 85. Unfortunately, she lost consciousness in the middle of the night in assisted care, and was rushed to the hospital by the staff. I made a mistake by asking the doctor's advice at that point. She said if it were her mother, she would do anything possible to save her life. Moreover, she informed me that, if I did refuse treatment, my mother would have to be moved to a nursing facility that same day. I was shocked by that, but I managed to persist in refusing treatment and found an unexpected ally in the hospital chaplain. The chaplain, also a woman, worked with the staff to keep my mother overnight. The decision to withdraw hydration the next day was the most difficult. Even though my mom had directed me to refuse all treatment,

I had a personal fear that thirst was a terrible way to die. I had to remind my-self constantly that my mother was not dying of thirst. She was dying of lung disease, and all I could do was prolong that dying, not make her well again.

Of course, you can't anticipate everything. There is always the un-expected: a new machine may be available; or an insurance provision can stump your healthcare agent. Talking about your preferences in a broader, more value-oriented way provides some principles for evaluating options as they arise. Is it important to you to die a "natural death"? There are social, emotional, and spiritual reasons why it might be. For some people, it's im-portant to see things through to the end. Others believe there's no reason to suffer unnecessarily. How do you feel about being conscious during the last days and weeks of your life? Would you prefer to be without pain at the end, even if it means being sedated?

Let's say you've been diagnosed with an aggressive kind of cancer. Would you take any opportunity to live a few more weeks or months? Or, if you are dying of lung disease, would you still want to receive antibiotics for pneumonia? You may want to be resuscitated if you suffer a first heart attack, but maybe not if you are dying of cancer when it happens. How important is it, if you are able to communicate, to do so until the very end of your life if you are able? Pain medications can make this difficult if not impossible.

You need to make clear to your healthcare agent how you feel about bringing the family into the discussion, and how you want to be treated if you can't communicate with them. How important is it that your wishes are carried out to the letter? Take the time to think through whether you want to make organ donations or, if the hospital or the family wants it, have an autopsy. Does it matter to you?

Communication About Your Prognosis

There are big cultural, social, and individual differences in what people want to know and what they are willing to tell others. The American Medical Association has mandated that physicians must not refuse to fully inform a patient about their diagnosis and prognosis, but that doesn't mean they have to tell you everything they think. As you might imagine, telling people they're going to die is very difficult, yet many physicians, especially oncologists, face this sensitive issue many times each year. Today, most doctors are committed to telling patients the full story of their diagnoses and the details of possible treatments, but they are reluctant to tell anyone definitively that their disease is terminal.

And, in a way, who knows how long a person actually has? A doctor may be able to tell you that almost everyone dies but be completely unable to predict how long you, in particular, have left to live. A terminal phase is often unpredictable, and it is not always clear that having a timetable is best for a patient. Full disclosure may help some patients and hurt others. Doctors are reluctant to prophesy and, as it turns out, they are often wrong when they do. Most often, they err on the side of optimism, overstating the amount of time people have left; but it also happens that some people outlive even the direst predictions.

Today anyone can go on the Internet and find out the average survival rates for any kind of disease. You can find detailed descriptions of symptoms and treatments. You can find personal accounts of people who are dying from a wide variety of diseases. Many Internet resources preface their discussion of prognoses with the warning that they will be presenting average lifespan data, and you might not want to read that. You have the right to know it, but you have to decide whether knowing every last detail is right for you.

In many cultures, families prefer to withhold some or all of the truth from a dying patient. On average, Caucasian Americans value self-direction and autonomy more than other racial and ethnic groups. Asians and Hispanics tend to believe that a stark prognosis is a burden to a patient and prefer to see how it rolls out as they days go by. In one study of Japanese doctors, for example, doctors often chose to speak to the family before telling the patient. There are cultures, some of them European, that prefer to withhold the truth about prognosis even with a diagnosis that the patient's condition is terminal. This includes Chinese, Japanese, and Korean families as well as

Ethiopian, Italian, Eastern European, and French families. Mexican families usually follow the lead of their physicians.

South and Central American families tend to be skeptical about giving a patient too much information, and there are also differences among cultural groups in terms of how they view life-sustaining procedures, organ donations, and autopsies. In some cultures and religions, people believe that the body will be reincarnated or resurrected in the afterlife and must, therefore, remain intact. Chinese and Japanese people consider the body a gift from their parents and are reluctant to donate organs or order autopsies. African Americans are more likely to make organ donations than many other groups but are often reluctant for spiritual reasons to suspend feeding or hydration. As in all things dying, there is no one best decision, no right way to do it.

Finally, we should discuss how to break the news to family and friends if you are diagnosed with a terminal illness. You don't need to tell anyone, and you certainly don't have to tell everyone everything.

Communicating With Family and Friends

In recent years, some writers have argued that, in the healthcare system, the pendulum has swung too far toward an emphasis on preferences, choice, and the autonomy of individuals. We've become too focused on procedures and medication rather than on the emotional, social, and spiritual aspects of life. Patients often care more about what family and friends think and feel than they do about their own experience. Family and friends often wish they could bear some of the pain and discomfort themselves. Mortal illness upsets the dynamics in the whole social system around a dying person. Social roles such as breadwinner, caregiver, lover, or playmate can disappear, and emotional roles such as "the strong one", "the decision maker," or "the good child" can change, causing confusion and stress for everyone. Many changes in family function and meanings occur. Consideration is due to the social and emotional stress of the network as well as that of the patient, if only because social networks can be crucial to maintaining hope and a fighting spirit, offering respite and just plain help to the family.

So how do you decide what to tell other people? It depends, of course, on the closeness of the relationship and the immediacy of the problems. The people closest—spouses, children, close relatives, and best friends—need to know the most. They need the chance to make contact in order to understand the needs of both the dying person and the family. People need to be able to express what the relationship has meant to them and to mend rifts or address misunderstandings. Perhaps the best way to break the news is suggested by the following guidelines doctors use: Think about time and place. Find a moment when you won't be interrupted or distracted. Begin at the beginning with what the family or friend already knows.

"You know I've been seeing a doctor about the problems I'm having breathing. Today I found out that the situation is quite serious. I've been diagnosed with stage 4 lung cancer." Keep it simple and straightforward, then take a moment to let the news sink in. Those on the other end of this conversation are likely to feel disoriented and shocked. "Are you kidding? I can't believe it," is a common first response. Don't be offended if people are unable to grasp what is happening to you.

"I'm having a hard time wrapping my head around it myself," might be the perfect reply. People will also ask you what else the doctor said. You can share the treatment plan and the options you are considering. Don't be afraid to admit that you are overwhelmed or in shock yourself.

It is common that friends and family respond to the announcement with a story of their own about someone they know who had this disease and got better. Sometimes, in their own shock, they tell you about someone who died of the same disease. It is hard to know how to respond to that. "I know I am in for a fight," might be appropriate, or just "Yes, I know that happens." Often friends make recommendations about what to do—get a second opinion, see this or that clinic or specialist, look into such and such a website. Simple responses such as "I'll put that on the list" or "I'll look into that; send me the information" are enough. For patients and their families, managing the reactions of others can be emotionally trying. Keeping it short and sweet will help.

As the facts sink in, people usually offer to help. "Let us know what we can do." That phrase usually signals that the discussion can be brought to a close. "I will, when I figure out what I need" is one way to handle the offer. You don't have to rack your brain to figure out what your friends can do at that moment, but it is also important to give it some thought. A friend might drive you to an appointment; take notes when you talk to the doctor; or help with food, laundry, or taking care of the kids. Most people are sincere in this offer. It's a way of expressing how much they care. For many patients and families, this can be a time of the "joy/pain." Researchers studying the Aztec language recently discovered an Aztec term for this complex experience, and it is a common feeling in our culture, too. You may discover how much you're loved and how many people are willing to help in the midst of your suffering. Dying is not all one thing. It is many things—not just fear, sadness, sorrow, and loss, but also a moment when people can appreciate the beauty of life, of the world, and of their relationships.

You don't have to do all of the talking yourself either. You may want to designate a point person or several point people to handle follow-up communication. It might be your spouse or an adult child. A good friend or a colleague at work can take on some of the burden. In the first few weeks especially, it's helpful to create an email or phone list that can be managed by someone else when you won't have the strength, either physically or emotionally, to tell people over and over again about the situation. If you are a friend or a family member, this is a good way to help. There are websites where you can share a blog, as Judy did when she was diagnosed with stage 3 colon cancer. You can find this blog under "cancer" at www.judystevenslong.wordpress.com.

Communicating With Children

The most difficult of all announcements, however, falls to those who have young children. It's important to recognize that even small children are deeply aware of the emotional life of their parents. They pick up all kinds of social signals and are acutely aware of changes in the attitudes and behaviors of family members. They need to know what's going on. Young children especially have a tendency to feel that everything happens because of something they did, or felt, or thought. They need reassurance on this point. Older children need more time than younger ones to prepare for the death of a parent. Children don't need to know every detail, but they need to know the general outline and how the family will be affected.

"We found out today that Daddy has a bad spot in his lungs and he needs to go into the hospital so the doctors can take it out. He'll be there for couple of days until he feels well enough to come home," might be enough in the beginning. Later, children should be kept updated on new developments that will affect how the parent feels or looks. "He's going to have a scar from here to here"; "He will have to have treatment to keep the spot from coming back"; "He might be pretty tired for a while or even lose some hair"; "He might be sick to his stomach, but that's just the medicine working." Be sure to ask if the child has any questions or worries, such as:"Is he going to die?"

At some point, when the answer is clear, this question must be answered honestly but, like a doctor giving a prognosis, you may not know for a long time. In the meanwhile, maintaining hope and a fighting spirit can be critical to everyone's well-being.

"The doctors and nurses will do everything they can to make sure that doesn't happen."

Helping children talk about their feelings allows them to feel cared for and to begin anticipatory grieving, a subject we'll cover at some length in Chapter 14. Children love to paint and draw, and that can be a good way for them to express some of their ideas and emotions. "Tell me about this picture," is a good way to begin a discussion. Try not to suggest an interpretation. Let children talk about what the drawing means to them. Use open-ended questions such as "Why is the dog crying?" rather than "Is the dog crying because of what happened to Daddy?" If a child is used to playing house or making up stories, those can serve as a good way into a child's inner life. Many hospitals, clinics, and hospices offer special programs for children who are coping with the death of a parent. It often helps for children to talk to other kids who are facing the same prospect or to an adult who has had the same experience as a child. Many hospice organizations offer special programs for children dealing with the death of a parent.

Families that cope well are families that seek resources and are able to express feelings and tolerate any differences that arise. Not everyone is going to feel the same way at the same time. Denial can be adaptive as long as it doesn't interfere with doing what needs to be done. There will be days when the situation is overwhelming and everybody melts down. There will be days that seem almost normal. You won't always have to have a "good attitude," and the research suggests that you don't have to, either. Depression, anger, fear, and sadness are normal reactions that come and go day to day. New information, such as how treatment is progressing, can restart the cycle of shock/recovery.

Families that stay focused on problems, look for solutions, and try different approaches are the families that survive the experience best, despite those days when everyone feels defeated and hopeless. "Hold out every hope and fight with every fiber," may be the best advice.

References for This Chapter:

Bryan M., & Ingpen, R. (1983). *Lifetimes: The beautiful way to explain death to children.* New York, NY: Bantam Books.

The Conversation Project Starter Kit. (2010). American Association of Family Physicians. http://www.aafp.org/patient-care/inform/conversation-project.html. Retrieved September 30, 2017.

Chapter 5

Patterns of Living and Dying:
Stages, Patterns, and Personality

The most widely publicized and influential account of the terminal stages of life is undoubtedly the work of Elizabeth Kübler-Ross. Almost everyone is familiar with her conclusion that people experience their own death in five characteristic stages. The first of these, *denial*, is dominated by shock and disbelief ("This isn't happening! There's been some mistake.")

After the shock wears off, *anger* sets in. A dying person can become angry at the doctors, at God or fate, even at friends and family ("Why me? I don't deserve this"). People sometimes become hostile with their caretakers, impatient with their children, and irritable over small, inconsequential things. Often, this stage is followed by *bargaining*. Dying people try to make a deal with God or fate, offering to be a better person, husband, or wife if they can live a little longer ("If I make it to Christmas, I'll be satisfied"). After Christmas, spring becomes the object of the bargain ("Just let me get through this winter").

When bargaining subsides, Kübler-Ross writes that "people begin to mourn themselves." She called this stage *depression*. Edward Shneidman, a founder of modern thanatology, believed mourning oneself is a sign of self-respect. A dying person mourns the loss of abilities, relationships, and experiences of function and well-being. Grief and sadness and feelings of distress and hopelessness mark this phase. Kübler-Ross claimed that patients who successfully negotiate the depression move on to *acceptance*.

In acceptance, patients report a sense of peace more often than despair or remorse. They become more detached from the outside world and the people in it. Kübler-Ross worked with many young adults and middle-aged people who were dying prematurely. She found they were more likely to continue feeling angry and to bargain with death longer than the elderly, who often feel that they have had long lives and do not feel cheated by death.

Kübler-Ross was a leader in the *death awareness movement* of the 1970s and 1980s, and she has certainly helped us all understand what kinds of emotions and reactions are likely to appear among dying people and their families. However, many researchers now believe the idea of linear stages is too simple. More recent evidence shows that people make a great variety of accommodations in response to a terminal diagnosis. It is also not clear that the pattern Kübler-Ross describes is optimal for everyone. In fact, it has been argued that practitioners have overused her stages to push patients toward "acceptance" and away from denial. Given that human beings are capable of many levels of awareness, terminally ill people cannot completely deny the fact that something is wrong. Knowledge and denial can oscillate rapidly and can even seem to occur simultaneously.

Patients are capable of denying certain aspects of their illness while accepting others. At the end of her life, Kübler-Ross was chronically ill herself, and she realized that all five phases can recur over the course of a long illness. She was often angry and frustrated. She mourned the loss of her independence but believed that she had, at the same time, accepted her own death.

In mainstream American culture, dying people are expected to do many things aside from attending to the reality of their prognosis. They are expected to manage the business of living as well. They still have to pay their bills, make logical decisions about medications and technology, and handle stressful relationships so that family and friends are able to remain close, all the while managing to do this with grace and dignity. The dying are expected to fight, not to withdraw and disengage. Given these impressive demands, it is no wonder that denial and acceptance fluctuate, not only in the person who is dying, but also in the social network surrounding the person.

Individual Differences

Some people don't want to talk about their imminent death, not because they're in denial, but because it's how they've handled difficulty throughout their lives. Some people withdraw. Some would rather die than suffer or cause suffering to those around them. Some become judgmental and intolerant while others open their arms and invite support. There may not be any one best way to die.

On the other hand, there may be some patterns that occur across groups. One way to think about this is to consider how personality types or styles might affect a person at the end of life. For example, Carl Jung talked about personality patterns that are universally recognized. He referred to these patterns as *archetypes* such as "the hero" or "the sage." He believed that there were archetypal patterns that can be recognized across cultures. One popularization of the idea of archetypes is found in the Enneagram, a list of personality patterns associated with certain characteristics.

There are nine Enneagram types. One of the types, the "reformer," sounds like a good match with the mainstream idea of a good death. A reformer is rational, idealistic, principled, purposeful, and self-controlled. Reformer types have all their ducks in a row, keep their fears to themselves, and carry on. The "helper" type is described as caring, demonstrative, generous, and people-pleasing. This might be the person who worries more about the suffering of friends and family than about their own suffering. The "investigator" is intense, perceptive, innovative, and secretive. An investigator might be the kind of person that sees the prospect of death as a final adventure. A list of these archetypes and a detailed description of each on is available at https://www.enneagraminstitute.com/type-descriptions/. Any of these patterns might help us understand the *pattern of dying* that a particular individual will take. Briefly, here are the nine major patterns:

1. THE REFORMER: The Rational, Idealistic type: Principled, Purposeful, Self-controlled, and perfectionistic.

2. THE HELPER: The Caring, Interpersonal Type: Demonstrative, Generous, People-Pleasing, and Possessive.

3. THE ACHIEVER: The Success-Oriented, Pragmatic Type: Adaptive, Excelling, Driven, and Image-Conscious.

4. THE INDIVIDUALIST: The Sensitive, Withdrawn Type: Expressive, Dramatic, Self-Absorbed, and Temperamental.

5. THE INVESTIGATOR: The Intense, Cerebral Type: Perceptive, Innovative, Secretive, and Isolated.

6. THE LOYALIST: The Committed, Security-Oriented Type: Engaging, Responsible, Anxious, and Suspicious.

7. THE ENTHUSIAST: The Busy, Fun-Loving Type: Spontaneous, Versatile, Distractible, and Scattered.

8. THE CHALLENGER: The Powerful, Dominating Type: Self-Confident, Decisive, Willful, and Confrontational.

9. THE PEACEMAKER: The Easygoing, Self-Effacing Type: Receptive, Reassuring, Agreeable, and Competent.

In the wake of Kübler Ross's work, many writers have offered ways to frame the terminal phase of life so that it provides a platform for both living and dying. One idea, put forward by Avery Weisman, has been called an *appropriate death*. An appropriate death is one that fulfills the patient's ideals and expectations, though it may not seem ideal to others. This suggests that there may different kinds of appropriate deaths, each congruent with the ideals and expectations of different kinds of people, as well as different patterns of dying preceding those deaths. For example, a person may deny a terrifying diagnosis, choose not to talk about options other than survival, and mobilize every possible resource to optimize the chance of "beating cancer." You might call this pattern the *path of the warrior* and see it as one common response. "Investigator" might be the Enneagram type of a person who would write a book like this.

Another useful construct offered by Weisman divides the terminal stage of life into three general phases: an *acute phase*, coinciding with the patient's initial awareness of the terminal condition, a *chronic living-dying phase*, in which the patient experiences anticipatory grief, and a *terminal phase*, beginning with the patient's final withdrawal from the outside world. Figure 5.1 presents a graphic representation of these three phases.

Figure 5.1

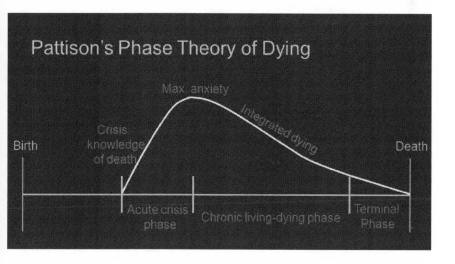

Different phases of dying call for different skills. Many dying people will not manage one stage well, but will do well in another. The acute phase requires people to maintain their strength and to grapple with understanding their disease and the responses of their own bodies. People in the acute phase have to cope with feelings of shock and anger, but still reach out for the resources that will sustain them through the chronic living-dying phase. As they move into the chronic phase, they must learn how to manage their symptoms and cope with uncertainty, stress, and suffering. In the final months or weeks, they have to deal with pain, disability, and loss of function. They need to sustain their relationships as long as they are able and say goodbye when the time comes. In addition, we may want them to develop as people and find meaning in this experience. That's a tall order. It requires courage, love and, above all, grit. Grit is a combination of passion and endurance that helps people overcome great obstacles.

Many of the phenomena described by Kübler-Ross occur in the first stage, the acute crisis. Patients and their families report a mix of shock, anxiety, anger, and bargaining. Later, during the chronic living-dying phase, they are more likely to feel fearful, lonely, and grief-stricken. Denial and acceptance can alternate or even happen simultaneously in any phase; furthermore, hope is possible in any phase, even when it is clear that recovery is impossible. For example, the patient can look forward to Christmas or Passover, to an anniversary, or to another spring. Hope allows people to better care for themselves and to maintain stronger relationships with those dear to them.

Denial can be adaptive by allowing people breathing room to adjust to a new reality; however, it can also prevent mobilization. Here we make a distinction between resistance and denial. People who resist dying are often sophisticated and resourceful. They don't dwell on death, instead finding meaning in life as it is. They discover ways to reframe what's going on and connect to those around them. There may still be things they want to accomplish. There can be ways for them to become more mature and figure out how to maintain their independence in the face of grief and anger. Emphasizing living does not mean that a person is unable to accept the inevitability of their own death. Remember, there is the warrior's way as well as the path of acceptance. Some writers, including Kübler-Ross, point out that the terminal phase of life offers opportunities for development and expression of the self in a way unbounded by convention.

Relating to a Dying Person: Healthcare Providers

As a society, we have gravitated toward the idea that people are entitled to know everything about their terminal illness whether or not they want to and that their family ought to know as well. There are two main objections to this position. First, people cannot cope without some sense of hope and, second, physicians and medical technicians aren't good at predicting how the illness of a particular person will progress. Progression often depends on age and on whether someone is otherwise in good health, is committed to the treatment plan outlined for them, and is willing to maintain a connection to life and to other people.

Most research shows that physicians and other healthcare personnel faced with patients who are dying aren't well prepared to relate to patients in the terminal phase of an illness. They are best at saving lives, at taking action, and at getting patients into treatment. Treatment providers can have trouble finding the proper distance from someone whom they cannot help or who does not respond well to treatment. They can feel confused, guilty, and defensive when it becomes clear that remission or cure is not possible. In fact, as we pointed out earlier, most of the literature suggests that doctors and nurses, along with first responders such as firefighters and police officers, harbor a stronger fear of death than most people.

Researchers have often found that, in the terminal phase of dying, patients and families may function more realistically than healthcare professionals, who can't give up until the very end, if ever. Patients who accept the challenge of fighting their terminal illnesses can benefit from a physician's tenacity in seeking new treatments and procedures. But it can be hard on a patient when a professional focuses too narrowly on a cure. A large section of the Institute of Medicine's 2015 report was devoted to research on the patient-physician relationship. There is, generally, far more information about this relationship than on any other aspect of the social system that surrounds a dying person.

Patients living with advanced illnesses experience significant distress stemming from the uncertainty of their future, from the decisions that must be made, and from the enormous changes that characterize their current situation. These may include the loss of occupational, social, and familial roles, as well as the ups and downs of the illness itself. Physicians often handle patients' emotions badly, rarely offering empathy, sticking instead to discussion of symptoms and treatments. Over time, patients learn not to express their fears and sorrows.

Women physicians do a bit better than men. They use more empathic language than do their male counterparts, as do nurses when compared to doctors. Many doctors see their roles as technical and scientific rather than social and emotional. Physicians often believe that discussing the end of life can rob patients and families of hope, but research offers no evidence that patients who know they are dying die any sooner that those who don't.

Perhaps physicians are uncomfortable with discussing end-of-life issues because they have trouble facing the limits of their ability to restore health and well-being or because they fear death themselves. Patients and healthcare agents, on the other hand, may want to discuss prognoses despite the uncertainty. They may want to be realistic and to make appropriate plans and decisions. The 2015 report of the Institute of Medicine endorsed shared decision making between the physician and the patient, although the report acknowledged that a history of paternalism makes that partnership a challenge.

Shared decision making means that the physician must take time to understand both the patient's perspective and the patient's social and emotional contexts. The patient's goals and preferences, as well as the role of the patient's family and healthcare agents, must be considered. People vary enormously in their feelings about participation in end-of-life care. Some much prefer to follow the lead of the physician, while others have strongly held beliefs about how the end of their lives should be managed. The research shows, however, that physicians often underestimate the ability and desire of patients to be involved in decision making. Patients who are well informed about their illnesses are more likely to file do-not-resuscitate orders with their physicians and less likely to die in a hospital. Patients' families may need to do their own research and make lists of questions that take full advantage of the physician's technical and scientific knowledge.

The need for good information is especially acute in the case of those who have been diagnosed with either heart disease or chronic obstructive pulmonary disease (COPD). Heart disease is unpredictable and raises the specter of sudden death. Heart patients often disregard end-of-life conversations once they've been released from the hospital or decline to have them in the first place. It is also difficult to establish a diagnosis or prognosis for a patient with heart failure, making the trajectory uncertain and the physician less apt to encourage a discussion. Patients with heart disease who do create advance directives are twice as likely to take advantage of hospice care as those who do not.

COPD is the third leading cause of mortality in the United States and the least well understood by patients. Many patients don't realize that COPD is a terminal condition and know nothing about what it might be like to die of COPD. COPD patients are only likely to attend to end-of-life planning when a crisis lands them in intensive care. Part of the problem here is that COPD is characterized by multiple acute events followed by periods of relative recovery. COPD is strongly related to smoking. Patients who smoke often feel shame and guilt and are less likely to face death head-on.

Although most cancer patients understand the potential lethality of their illness, they also undergo extensive treatments that could last from a few weeks to years, making it easy to put off the discussion of end of life. Many deny that they are terminally ill because the trajectory may be long, with periods during which the progress of the disease slows or even goes into remission. Advance care planning is associated with less use of heroic measures, fewer admissions to intensive care, and earlier enrollment in hospice or palliative care. Hospice and palliative care are, in turn, associated with improved quality of life for both patients and caregivers.

Hardest of all and least well understood is the plight experienced by patients afflicted by dementia and by their families. The Centers for Disease Control estimates nearly one-half of Americans over 85 have dementia and lack the capacity to make decisions for themselves. It's hard to underestimate the importance of end-of-life planning for those who will be incapacitated by this set of disorders, which includes some rare diseases such as Huntington's chorea. Dementia often leads to the loss of support from family or friends because one's behavior becomes so unpredictable, repetitive, or distressing. Advance planning is especially critical early on in the progression of the disease. When healthcare agents understand the complications of advanced dementia and its poor prognosis, they are far less likely to choose life-extending procedures or repeated hospitalizations.

Caregivers

The Institute of Medicine has reported that an estimated 66 million Americans, or almost 30% of the adult population, are caregivers, and that the vast majority of them are women. In 2011, the value of caregiving services provided by family members was estimated to be $450 billion. Caregivers provide an average of 20 hours of service per week and face significant stress in their daily lives. Their duties may include administering medications, maintaining complex equipment, and the feeding, bathing, and toileting of an ill family member. They also need to make sure that the patient is dressed, groomed, and driven to appointments. Most caregivers serve a dying person without formal training, and few of them receive support in managing their own fears, especially when the patient is a child.

Caregivers must also manage their own lives, meeting the physical, emotional, and spiritual needs of the dying patient as well as meeting responsibilities to other family members. The financial toll on caregivers can be devastating when they must take time off of work, when there are high out-of-pocket medical expenses, or when the breadwinner is the patient. The Institute points out that modern families are smaller than they were for most of history, that more women work outside the home, and that people live much longer after they become ill. The situation is expected to worsen over the next 15 years as the number of people who are 45 to 64 years old decreases relative to the number of people in their 80s. In 2010, there were seven people aged 45–64 for every person in their 80s. By 2030, the ratio will be only four to one. This means there will be fewer people to provide care in the coming years.

Caregivers need to be adaptive and resilient in the face of exhausting work. They are also at increased risk of disease because they don't do well at taking care of themselves; they eat poorly and lose sleep because of all the problems they face. These problems only worsen as the patient moves from the chronic into the terminal phase. If families try to share responsibilities for a patient who is difficult or extremely ill, the patient may be moved from one home to another, which can be hard on the patient and make coordination of care more problematic.

Family caregivers have received some protection from the federal government. The Family Medical Leave Act of 1993 guarantees up to 12 weeks of job-protected, unpaid leave when caring for a parent, spouse, or child. Medicaid programs in some states offer small sums for home-care services provided by family members, as does the VA Program for caregivers of seriously injured veterans. During the last six months of life, hospice can provide respite and emotional and social support for caregivers. Despite this, few families feel comfortable with hospice care until the very last few weeks, so hospice care is often not well utilized.

The Wider Circle

Sometimes patients feel overwhelmed by too much attention, causing conflict with family and friends who are searching for ways to support them. The question "How are you doing?" repeated over and over can be tiring and ultimately irritating. Family and friends reaching out can make an important difference, but it's also important to remember that the patient may not be in a place to respond. One piece of advice is to stay in the present. Rather than ask an open-ended question like "How are you?" it can be helpful to keep it in the present by asking, "How are you doing today?" or "How do you feel right now?"

If you write an email or send a text message, make it an affirmation rather than a question. "Thinking about you and hoping you're having the best possible day"; "Love you and holding you in my thoughts today." Yes, it sounds like a greeting card. It's okay. You don't have to be creative. Try not to make suggestions and recommendations, but offer an opportunity for communication without demanding a response. If the person responds to your note, you might talk about alternatives or treatment, but don't force it. Let the patient guide the length and depth of the communication. It *is* hard to know what to say and it's okay to say that, too. Sometimes just your touch or gesture can be enough. Try to put aside your expectations and see what the prognosis means to the patient. Keep it simple. Here are some suggestions from the Center for Living and Dying. You can access their website at https://www.thecenterfordyingandliving.org/.

1. Be honest about your own thoughts, concerns, and feelings.

2. When in doubt, ask questions:

    How is that for you?

    How do you feel right now?

    Can you tell me more about that?

    Am I intruding?

    What do you need?

    What are the ways you can take care of yourself?

3. When you are responding to a person facing a crisis situation, use statements such as:

    I feel _____

    I believe _____

    I would want _____

    rather than statements that may not give the person the opportunity to express unique needs and feelings, such as:

    You should _____

    That's wrong.

    Everything will be okay.

4. Stay in the present as much as possible.

    How do you feel *right now*?

    What do you need *right now*?

5. Listening can be profoundly healing. You don't have to make it better. You don't have to have the answers. You don't have to take the pain away. It's the patient's pain. Patients need to experience it in their own time and in their own way,

6. People in crisis need to know that they have decision-making power. It may be appropriate to point out alternatives.

7. Offer any practical assistance you feel comfortable giving.

As a friend or a relative of the family, it makes some sense for you to offer specific kinds of help rather than waiting for someone to ask. Caregivers are often so overwhelmed that they don't have time to think about what kind of help they need, much less to figure out who might be available. "Let me make up some meals you can freeze and take out when you don't have time to cook," is usually a helpful gesture. "Can I drive him to his appointments this week?" is another, as is "Why don't you send the kids over to play with my kids after school on Tuesdays and Thursdays?" Specific offers in the present—this week or this month—are most likely to be accepted.

Sometimes the biggest help to dying people and their families is an open mind and a listening heart. "Do you have time for a walk this week?"; "Can I bring you a box of cookies?"; "How has the radiation gone this week?" These are all ways to signal that you're available to talk. Try to be simple and specific. Don't make suggestions or question what a caregiver does or feels. Don't argue or proselytize or second guess. Try to repeat what the other person says in your own words. Ask the other person how he or she feels about something that's going on. Be present. Be centered. Be accepting.

References for This Chapter:

Daniels, D., & Price, V. (2009). *Essential enneagram: The definitive personality test and self-discovery guide: Revised & Updated.* New York, NY: Harper Collins.

Duckworth, A. (2016). *Grit: The power of passion and perseverance.* New York, NY: Simon and Schuster.

Pattison, E. M. (1977). *The experience of dying.* Englewood Cliffs, NJ: Prentice-Hall Inc.

Weisman, A. T. (1972). *On dying and denying: A psychiatric study of terminality.* Ann Arbor, MI: University of Michigan Press.

CHAPTER 6

SPECIAL CIRCUMSTANCES: SUDDEN OR TRAUMATIC DEATH, AND ASSISTED DYING

It's hard to describe what happens when someone close to you dies in a traumatic way, whether by accident, natural disaster, murder, or suicide. People often can't remember exactly what happened or how it happened, although many may be haunted by vivid images that seem frozen in time. For survivors, the experience is often accompanied by a variety of symptoms from memory loss to dissociation. *Dissociation* is defined as a feeling of detachment from reality, which can vary from feeling as if you're watching a movie of your life to periods of feeling detached, not only from external events, but also from inner experience. A trauma is an experience that disrupts one's sense of self in the world, and it can cause long-term emotional problems.

Survivors may develop post-traumatic stress disorder (PTSD), serious depression, addictive behaviors, or anxiety and panic attacks. There's no way to predict how traumatic death will affect the survivor. Some people develop full-blown mental health disorders such as borderline or bipolar personality disorder, schizoaffective disorder, or intense phobias. Trauma destabilizes and fragments one's sense of self. Feelings of self-blame, self-loathing, and shame can stand in the way of recovery. When a person's sense of safety is challenged, it can leave them unable to engage in intimate relationships and make it difficult to trust other people enough to accept comfort and support. Survivors often relive their feelings of terror and helplessness over and over again. This is especially true for soldiers and civilians in war zones and for victims of mass violence or natural disasters.

Our world is fraught with stories of violence and disaster. Many nations, including our own, have been plagued by violence and terrorism, from planes flying into buildings to shootings, stabbings, and bombings. We all imagine what it would be like to be sprayed with bullets at a concert or trapped at the top of a building that's on fire. We think about what we would do in a tornado, a hurricane, or a tsunami. Children and adults can develop overwhelming fears and phobias when they're caught in such events. It's often difficult to avoid seeing and hearing about the worst moments on radio, television, and social media. Many writers have argued that conditions such as these produce a kind of psychological disorder in the culture and change the meaning of the self. People can feel inconsequential, and human life can seem meaningless in an unpredictable world.

Any time death occurs unexpectedly, survivors have a more difficult time coping. A deadly heart attack or a massive stroke causes survivors to wonder whether they could've done something differently ("Should I have called 911 sooner?") or to feel guilty ("I didn't get a chance to tell him how much he meant to me"). If the circumstances are grim enough, grief may be prolonged for years or remain unresolved for the rest of a person's life. Guilt, shame, and self-doubt are especially likely when someone close commits suicide.

Suicide

Suicide is particularly hard for survivors partly because of the stigma it carries. It is seen as a sin in Christianity and Judaism and a as crime under Islamic law, despite the number of suicide bombers sanctioned by extremist groups. Suicide was a felony in many places in the United States until just before the turn of the twentieth century. Today, suicide still carries the stigma of mental illness. The focus of research on suicide is almost always on prevention and intervention. Suicide is not okay in this society. It can cause endless difficulties for survivors who may try to cover it up, be unwilling to talk about it, or be in denial about it ("It was an accidental overdose"). The current epidemic of opioid addiction in the U.S. exists a he intersection of suicide and accidental death.

Suicide can haunt survivors for years, especially the parents of a hild or an adolescent who commits suicide. Parents may suffer accusations nade not only by themselves, but also by other family members and even riends, not to mention by people who don't even know the family. When hildren and adolescents commit suicide, it becomes a community event, ppearing in the local paper and motivating the creation of grief groups r other special interventions at the school. The burden is all the greater ecause often no one knows exactly what happened or why. Survivors feel epressed, guilty, angry, or confused, depending on how they frame the circumstances from one moment to the next. The suddenness of the event can elay acceptance of the death, evoking fresh grief every time it comes up.

The problems of survivors are exacerbated by the definition of suicide as the act of carrying out the intention of killing oneself. There are many vay to hasten one's own death, through refusing to take medication properly r taking medication with alcohol. Lifestyle issues such as smoking, obesi-y, and the recreational use of drugs and alcohol can take years off a person's fe. Should this be considered a kind of suicide? Do people who do these ings intend to harm themselves? Do they just not care or live in denial that teir behavior will actually shorten their lives? In *A Commonsense Book of Death*, the well-known thanatologist Edwin Shneidman makes a distinction etween intentional death, unintentional death, and *subintentional death*.

Intentional Death includes several different patterns:

- a death seeker who wishes cessation of life

- a death initiator who believes he/she will die soon and wants control

- a death ignorer who believes he/she won't really experience cessation

- a death darer who takes big gambles

Unintentional death includes a number of patterns, too:

- a death welcomer is usually an old person with a long illness

- a death acceptor is resigned to his/her destiny

- a death postponer tries to stay alive

- a death disdainer feels above dying, like many teens

- a death feigner engages in manipulative suicide attempts

A subintentional death is characterized by unconscious movement toward death that may include drugs, drink, neglect, and accident proneness

- a death chancer courts death

- a death hastener lives an unhealthy lifestyle or mismanages his/her own health

- a death facilitator allows death to happen

- a death capitulator gives into death, as in voodoo deaths

- a death experimenter tries to lower his/her level of consciousness, as with drugs

According to the American Foundation for the Prevention of Suicide, suicide is the tenth leading cause of death in the United States. More than 44,000 people commit suicide every year. Guns are used in nearly half of all suicides. Three times more men commit suicide than women, and suicide rates peak twice over the life span, once at ages 54–64, and again after age 85. Suicide rates are highest for Caucasians and Native Americans; African Americans and Asian/Pacific Islanders have the lowest rates of suicide of any racial or ethnic group. The saddest statistic from the Centers for Disease Control notes that, between 2007 and 2015, suicide rates doubled for girls aged 15–20, and suicide rates for children aged 10–14 also doubled during that same period.

Children who commit suicide often do so impulsively over family problems or rejection by friends or, in adolescence, rejection by a boyfriend or girlfriend. Children who've been diagnosed with attention deficit hyperactivity disorder (ADHD) are at particular risk. Many younger children don't yet understand that death is irreversible. Though they may have the idea that they'll be able to see that people are sorry after they are dead, they can't imagine the grief that others will suffer, and they don't understand how disastrous their death may be a for their families.

Diane is a middle-aged mother who struggled with the suicide of her 12-year-old daughter. She spent weeks in shock, devastated by grief, finally trying to pull herself together again by doing "normal things," such as grocery shopping, and going to the bank or the post office. About a month after her daughter died, Diane visited Costco, where she had shopped for over a decade. Though she felt okay when she entered the store, got a basket, and started down the aisles, suddenly, in the middle of the store, she was completely disoriented. She didn't know where she was or what she was there for. She stood stock-still while people rushed around her and her cart. Then all the psychotherapy she had been undergoing kicked in, and she understood that this was another grief reaction. She began to talk herself off the ledge. She said to herself, "It's okay, honey; just breath and stand still. After about 10 minutes, she remembered where she was, and was able to return to her grocery shopping.

Her story is not unusual; many people experience situations like this after a traumatizing death, but they don't expect it, and think they are losing their minds. Counseling can offer strategies for talking oneself through the worst of it.

Research suggests that suicides among young adults are related to feeling trapped and hopeless, withdrawing from friends and family, and increased use of drugs and alcohol. In fact, alcohol is a factor in about 30% of all suicides. Most adults also give verbal signals that they're deeply troubled before attempting suicide, but those signs can be sidelong and subtle. "I'd just as soon not wake up tomorrow"; "Everyone would be better off without me"; "I don't know if I can live like this anymore."

Suicide among the elderly may be even more frequent than the statistics suggest because older people who are in frail health or severely depressed may simply stop taking care of themselves, fail to take critical medicine, or take too much of it. Autopsies are seldom done on people in end-stage diseases, especially if they die in the hospital. Older men in particular can suffer from feelings of meaninglessness after they lose the major roles on which their self-esteem depended or when they feel immobilized and confined by their illness. In the box below, Kjell Rudestam, an internationally known expert on traumatic death, describes rare, but deeply traumatic, cases of murder-suicide.

An Expert talks about Suicide

The loss of a family member or friend results in predictable grief in the form of significant sadness and emotional upset. However, when the source of that loss is suicide, survivor reactions are compounded and are likely to go beyond feelings associated with normal grief. These include pronounced guilt ("Could I have prevented it?"; "Am I not worth living for?"), shame (the stigmatizing nature of suicide in most cultures), anger ("How dare he/she punish us like this?"), and confusion. Whereas some acts of suicide are predictable and even anticipated, in most cases the search to make sense of what appears to be a senseless act is played out over a long period of time among the survivors of suicide loss. An even more devastating event is a murder-suicide, where the perpetrator of the murder subsequently ends his or her life. Fortunately, murder-suicides are relatively rare, comprising about 5% of all homicidal deaths. But their legacy among families, friends, and even communities endures. Such events challenge our basic trust in the fabric of society and create multiple victims in their wake. Anyone who has either witnessed or been close to a murder-suicide is apt to have a traumatic reaction wherein the event becomes replayed and reimagined in both waking images and disrupted sleep cycles. Family members of the murderer experience not only a direct loss from the suicide, but also inherit the pain of trying to understand the deliberate taking of another life, usually leading to pronounced feelings of guilt, shame, and even responsibility for the murder itself. Those most impacted by the original victim's death are likely to feel rage and anger at the murderer and a complicated grief reaction of their own. In addition to experiencing profound grief and mind-numbing confusion, they often find themselves in the middle of loyalty conflicts within the larger family system.

Medically-Assisted Dying

In 1997, the State of Oregon passed death-with-dignity legislation, allowing physicians to prescribe a lethal dose of medication to terminally ill patients who have persistently expressed a desire to die and are within six months of a natural death. This prognosis must be certified by a physician or, in some states, by two physicians. Washington, Vermont, and California have also passed such laws. In Montana, the court ruled that physician assistance in suicide should not be held illegal. In all of these states, patients must administer the medication themselves. Neither a physician nor any other person may help the patient take a lethal dose. In Oregon, the Supreme Court upheld the law after a long legal battle.

These laws were passed after much ethical discussion and debate, given that the primary role of the physician is to save lives, not to end them. While the American Medical Association has not supported this *Right to Die* movement, it has taken the position that the use of *sedation to unconsciousness* is permissible when no other options are effective in controlling pain and discomfort. Many writers have argued that permitting assisted suicide is the first move down a "slippery slope" that could end in the euthanasia of people who are seen as either undesirable or a burden to society. Those who take this position believe that if hospice, do-not-resuscitate orders, and palliative care were widely used, and people had adequate health insurance to pay for good care, there might be little or no need for assisted suicide.

The Right to Die movement in the United States is seeking to advance death-with-dignity legislation in many states. People in the movement talk about "self-deliverance" rather than suicide. They point out that where assisted suicide has been legalized there are many safeguards against the slippery slope. For example, in 2015 California passed legislation that requires the patient to request assistance in dying on two separate occasions at least two weeks apart, with the second one being in writing. The physician must certify that the patient would otherwise die within six months and is not suffering from mental illness.

In 2016, 191 people completed the protocol for receiving lethal doses of medication in California, and 111 actually purchased the drugs.

Most of those who did so were older cancer patients who were enrolled in hospice/palliative care and were covered by insurance. These data conflict with the position that adequate care would prevent assisted suicides. Furthermore, in the Netherlands, where there is universal healthcare, some people still choose assisted suicide. Right to Die supporters use information such as this to argue that hospice, palliative care, and universal healthcare coverage will not meet the needs of all patients who are struggling with end-stage diseases.

A Gallup poll from 2016 showed that six in 10 people in the U.S. support the Right to Die movement and that attitudes toward it have become increasingly positive over the past 50 years. Men are more likely than women to favor it, as are those with more education and more liberal political opinions. The vast majority of physicians, however, appear unwilling to facilitate an assisted suicide. In 2000, an article in the *Journal of the American Medical Association* reported that, while 60% of physicians (about the same percentage as the general population) were in favor of legalizing assisted suicide, only 10% would seriously consider participating.

The same article reported that older patients who feel appreciated are less likely to be interested in assisted suicide, especially if they are African American or religious. Those who express the desire to die are those who need the most burdensome care and who experience the most pain and discomfort, especially dyspnea (difficulty in breathing). Depression and feelings of hopelessness are also more frequent in those who wish to die, confounding the situation because some current laws require the physician to certify that the patient is not depressed.

Among caregivers, those who feel most burdened are also most likely to support Right to Die legislation. Researchers have not found any relationship between the caretaker's assessment of the patient's pain and his or her support for assisted suicide. Few caretakers, however, are willing to assist a patient who is attempting to commit suicide. Extrapolating their finding to the general population, the authors projected that, while 250,000 people would consider assisted suicide if it were generally legal in the United States, only 100,000 would discuss it with anyone. Moreover, very few of them—fewer than 10,000—would actually take a lethal dose of medication. In the Netherlands, where it is completely legal and physicians are allowed to administer lethal injections, only 3.4% have taken advantage of the law.

It is surprising that, given the complexity of the ethical issues and the current trend toward legalization, there is no information we can find about the effect of physician-assisted suicide on survivors. Certainly there may be lasting psychological and emotional consequences for caretakers, who are already experiencing the greatest burdens, if they advocate in favor of the patient's assisted suicide. More research on this topic seems especially crucial as the Right to Die movement spreads across the United States.

Homicide

Homicide is perhaps the most traumatic of all deaths, especially when it happens to someone who was young and healthy or in the prime of their lives. Murder is complicated by fear of the perpetrator, legal repercussions, and autopsy. It is particularly haunting when a child is killed. Whether the victim is a child or an adult, though, the family must cope with police investigations, lawyers, court dates, and media over long periods, during which the shock, anger, and grief may erupt as new information comes to light or details are revealed. Survivors who weren't present at the scene may conjure up horrible images about what happened and be unable to stop their ruminations.

If the murderer is caught and convicted, once a sentence is served, the family may have to face parole hearings every year. Families can lose faith in the system or even in humanity itself. Fear and anger can persist for years in survivors and may never completely resolve. As many as three-quarters of homicide victims knew the perpetrator. When this happens, guilt and blame spread among friends and family, who feel that they should have been able to prevent the crime or that another person close to the victim contributed to the crime.

The penalties for murder are likely to be less severe when it occurs in intimate relationships. Part of the reason for this may lie in the perception that murder in families is too complex or emotionally charged to be fully understood and that the murderer does not pose threat to the community as a whole. The perpetrator may only be charged with manslaughter, for example. For survivors, a lesser sentence can intensify anger, guilt, and fear. Murder committed by a stranger is more likely to disrupt the neighborhood, causing fear and distress and affecting nearby businesses or community spaces such as parks or schools. Such murders usually results in higher penalties than those that occur in families or close relationships.

Sudden or Accidental Death

Sudden or accidental death is a leading cause of death among children and young adults. The impact on survivors is intensified by the abruptness of such a death and its theft of so many years. Adult survivors, especially spouses with children, are likely to develop social, emotional, and even physical problems that persist over prolonged periods. Young widows and widowers feel cheated and angry. They are quite likely to feel guilty, as well. The "What if I had only. . ." question haunts them. Young survivors can suffer from a variety of symptoms and mental health problems, from feeling a loss of identity to acute bursts of "searching and longing." They can feel disoriented and may even feel that they are going crazy for weeks, even months.

Seldom, of course, have young people who die made any arrangements, leaving finances and personal relationships in disarray. When young parents die, families often suffer a loss of a breadwinner as well as the loss of a caretaker, because young marrieds tend to share both roles. On the other hand, younger people are more resilient. They usually find the strength to work through their grief and build a new independent life. When a young parent dies, the children require special attention. The remaining spouse may feel overwhelmed and outraged at his or her fate. The children also feel a terrible loss, and their hardship can be intensified by the grief of the living parent. The strength of the family's social network and their access to emotional and financial resources are pivotal to a surviving child's recovery.

The traumatic death of a parent can cause children to have horrifying thoughts and images, causing them to suppress all thoughts of the parent who died and making it more difficult to cope with their grief. Family cohesion is central to helping children overcome such trauma. Families need to come together, allow time for grief and recovery, express love and commitment to each other, and try to stay open and flexible. Professional help is usually a good idea, and it's often available from community organizations and schools.

Natural Disasters, Mass Trauma, and War

Exposure to community violence, war, terrorism, extreme weather events, earthquakes, and wildfires have become part of everyday life in the global village. Large-scale disasters can stretch the resources of even well-prepared institutions such as the Federal Emergency Management Administration (FEMA) or the Red Cross. After the 9/11 attack, people of all ages, even those living in California and Washington, far from the Twin Towers, felt traumatized by the incessant television replay of the planes hitting the towers. Many children thought that each replay was a new incident.

We have few studies of how people cope with and overcome the trauma of extreme events. Often, there is public solidarity and mourning, and that can help. Educational institutions, hospices, and organizations such as the Red Cross, along with disaster-response teams from organizations such as the American Psychological Association, offer bereavement services and trauma support, but there is little evidence showing whether these interventions are effective. Evidence does suggest, however, that returning to normal routines as soon as possible, including going back to school and to work, restores calm and helps people feel stable and secure again.

Traumatic death, in all of its forms, can shake the basic beliefs people hold about whether their own culture can provide security and continuity in life. Perhaps one of the most important things a person can do to recover from trauma is to create a narrative that restores a sense of meaning and control. People often need to go over and over every detail of the death, weaving a story that explains how such a thing could happen and finding ways to integrate it into the larger narrative of their lives. The patience of friends, family, and professional caregivers can make all the difference. Listening with compassion, withholding judgment, and providing a space for the survivor to do this kind of personal work can make huge contributions to healing.

References for This Chapter:

Emanuel, E. J., Fairclough, D. L., Emanuel, L. L. (2000). Attitudes and desires related to euthanasia and physician-assisted suicide among terminally ill patients and their caregivers. *JAMA, 284*(19): 2460-2468. doi:10.1001/jama.284.19.2460

Shneidman, E. (2008). *A commonsense book of death.* Plymouth, MA: Rowman & Littlefield.

CHAPTER 7

ADDRESSING THE STATE:
FORMS AND LEGAL MATTERS

In an earlier chapter, we outlined some of the issues people face when they engage in a conversation about how they want to die. In this chapter, we tackle the legal forms for making those preferences known. Forms and instruments may seem boring and difficult, but the social and emotional consequences of not attending to them make it harder for those we leave behind. Things can go awry in families where there are no guidelines for the raft of decisions that must be made when someone is terminally ill.

One of the simplest ways to record your preferences for your end of life is to use a form called a *living will*. A living will does not spell out all of the procedures and treatments, as do the more complex California Advanced Directives that we discussed in Chapter 4. It does allow you to state a general desire to die without the use of the types of machines and treatments that keep a body alive without the prospect of the underlying disease going into remission or being cured. In all states, a physician ultimately determines whether or not a treatment is curative, so in order for the form to take effect, at least one physician, sometimes two, must agree that nothing can be done to ensure your recovery before the terms of the will come into effect. An example of a living will can be found in Appendix 1.

A living will allows you to designate a healthcare agent who can make decisions for you if you're incapacitated. This is sometimes called a "healthcare proxy," and your agent may not substitute his or her own judgment to override your preferences if you've stated them clearly. Of course, there are multiple problems with this idea. If you're unconscious, could an agent ignore your preferences if a new treatment is suggested, one that might or might not promote your recovery? Can your agent enroll you in an experimental treatment that you can no longer evaluate? About 40% of all terminal patients are unable to make decisions for themselves in the last few days or weeks of their lives.

Many decisions depend on the degree of pain and discomfort the physician or healthcare agent believes a patient is experiencing. For instance, your agent could decide that you're in great pain and should be given more medication, even if it causes you to become continuously unconscious. But how can anyone ever know the discomfort of another person, especially if that person isn't lucid much of the time? Conversations about how much suffering one can stand are rare indeed. No one wants to contemplate their own suffering in much detail.

Even if you could discuss all the possibilities with your healthcare agent or physician, a living will must be made available to the hospital or nursing home. It must be part of the medical record to be fully enforced. Even if the hospital, the agent, and the physician have it, a living will does not cover procedures such as cardiopulmonary resuscitation (CPR) that are used by emergency medical technicians (EMTs). In fact, EMTs are required to perform CPR until the patient is revived or declared dead by a physician at the hospital. Recently, writers in the field have begun to argue that CPR is now overused, causing more suffering for the dying patient, whose ribs may be broken in the process. Once a patient is at the emergency room, doctors are usually reluctant to discontinue CPR and allow the patient to die without express instructions to do so. Many physicians are not comfortable watching a patient die in front of them, and families are also reluctant to let that happen.

One legal document that covers some of the shortcomings of living wills and do-not-resuscitate (DNR) orders is called the Physicians Orders for Life-Sustaining Treatment (POLST), which is available in many states. It can be used to inform EMTs and can follow a patient to a nursing home if the patient is transferred from the hospital. POLSTs are medical orders that must be signed by a health professional, usually a physician, although in some states a nurse practitioner or a physician's assistant can sign. Because these are actual medical orders, EMTs and facilities such as nursing homes will honor them. POLSTs are legally binding and actionable, which means a suit can be brought if they are ignored. Of course, EMTs and others must see them in order to honor them. They have to be posted in plain sight—on the front door or refrigerator, carried in a wallet, or indicated on a bracelet.

Filling out an advance directive or a living will, filing a DNR with the physician and the hospital, discussing your preferences with your health-care agent, and posting POLST orders are the safest ways to ensure that your wishes are followed. These documents require thoughtfulness, persistence, and follow-up. Furthermore, if you change your mind, they must be revised. These documents need to be reviewed and updated from time to time. How you feel about treatment when you're young may change when you're older and have a terminal illness. In any situation where outcomes must be predicted, physicians are less likely to attend to old documents and preferences. This is especially true in cases that involve cognitive impairment. Physicians are less likely than patients to consider mental awareness in making life-sustaining choices.

The forms we've discussed so far primarily concern the patient's physical and mental condition. They focus on pain, cognitive function, and the possibility of recovery. Another document, known as *Five Wishes*, addresses quality-of-life and spiritual matters, as well as the practical matters included in most advance directives. It allows you to specify the treatments you do or do not want and to name a healthcare agent, as do the other forms, but it also covers issues such as how important it is to you to be well groomed, comfortable, without pain, and able to care for your own intimate needs. It allows you to express your preference for dying at home or in a hospice. The final section deals with what you want your loved ones to know about arranging a funeral or memorial service and how you want them to deal with your body. It gives you a chance to write down your thoughts about spiritual matters such as love, forgiveness, and meaning. Once the first two wishes about treatment and your choice of a healthcare agent are signed and witnessed, they become legal documents.

Fives Wishes has been criticized for the underlying assumption that the person wishes to die a natural death, creating a bias against physician-assisted suicide. The key sentence on the form is "I do not want anything done or omitted by my doctors or nurses with the intention of taking my life." You can simply cross this out if you want to use the rest of the form but don't necessarily agree that a natural death is of paramount importance to you. None of these documents can cover every situation that might arise; however, each of them offers an opportunity to think through these issues and discuss them with your family, your doctor, and your healthcare agent. The more they know about what you think and feel, the more likely it is that they'll make good choices for you in unexpected circumstances.

Autopsy and Organ Donation

An autopsy is a dissection and analysis of the body and can include a variety of tests such as x-rays and biopsies, toxicological tests of blood and urine, as well as tissue cultures that might reveal infections. In most cases of natural death, an autopsy is unnecessary. A coroner or medical examiner may order one if the cause of death is unknown or suspicious. Local laws often require an autopsy if the death was unexpected or traumatic. Autopsies may also be required when legal issues arise about the role of doctors, staff, or hospitals in a person's death or to help researchers understand more about a particular disease or the effects of the treatment.

Unless the law requires an autopsy or the deceased has donated his or her body for research, an autopsy may not be performed without the consent of the next of kin. Because autopsies are rarely required, few hospitals now have the facilities to complete them. Families seeking information about either the cause of death or evidence of hereditary diseases may have to engage a private autopsy service. Autopsies can be used in court to settle a variety of issues, including questions about medical or criminal liability.

If a dying person has approved an organ donation, there are few legal or ethical issues. However, organs that are donated must be harvested quickly, and the procedures can be upsetting for survivors who have just experienced the death of a loved one. The Uniform Anatomical Gift Act (2006) provides a list of persons who can authorize a donation if the deceased has not expressed a preference. It's very difficult to override a person's decision to donate an organ, and most hospitals have procedures in place to encourage and carry out donations.

The need for transplants has increased dramatically, as more people either become newly eligible for donations or have, despite having other significant health issues, managed to outlive an earlier transplant. In some countries, people have to opt out of organ donation if they do not want to participate. As the population ages and deaths from automobile accidents decline because of safety standards and new equipment, there are also fewer donors.

The pressure for organ donations to be accomplished quickly can erupt in legal battles between medical examiners who need to autopsy a body and organ-procurement agencies. New procedures also allow organs to be harvested from donors who are not totally brain dead but have suffered cardiac death. Such procedures are a challenge to state laws that require total brain death before an organ can be removed. Families can also raise legal issues about whether a patient meets the criteria for brain death and, as mentioned in Chapter 2, they are often confused by the bewildering use of machines that are required to preserve organs once someone is pronounced dead.

The National Kidney Foundation (2002) offers a list of rights for donor families that might assist them in making decisions and in coping with the emotional outcome of those decisions. According to the foundation, families have a right to expect that the hospital staff will both treat the donor's body with respect and provide the family with information about how the organs were used. Families ought to be provided with information about the condition of the recipient and, if possible, be given an opportunity to contact the recipients of the organs. This list of rights also includes bereavement support for the family and a way to contact other donor families.

Inheritance: Wills, Trusts, and Probate

The person for whom a will is prepared is called the *testator*. Wills often cover the testator's preferences about end-of-life decisions. Wills or companion documents designate a healthcare agent and expressly state whether or not the person intends to make organ donations. Of course, the will also details the person's estate and lays out how the estate is to be distributed among the beneficiaries.

After a person dies, most wills must go through a probate. Probate simply refers to the legal process whereby the wishes of the deceased are carried out, the estate is distributed, and bills and taxes are paid. Most states require that people be, at the time they create a will, at least 18 years old and able to make rational decisions. Wills must be written down and witnessed, although some states allow a will to be made orally in the case of imminent death or fear of mortal injury. For instance, in some states, testators who are likely to die before they can be extricated from an automobile accident may make an oral will to someone who is present.

About half of the states in the U.S. also recognize the validity of a *holographic will* under some conditions. A holographic will is written out entirely by the hand of the testator. In most states that allow holographic wills, they must be witnessed, except in clear emergencies or in the case of soldiers in armed conflict. Some, though, don't even require witnesses as long as it can be proved that the deceased actually wrote the will. Legalzoom.com provides a current list of states that recognize holographic wills. For more information about holographic wills, go to www.legalzoom. com.

Wills can also establish testamentary trusts that specify conditions for the distribution of an estate. For example, a sum of money may be put in trust for minor children until they reach age 18. Testators may distribute their estates any way they choose, but if they exclude a spouse or dependent children, there may be a legal challenge that could overturn the will. Some states clearly require that spouses and dependent children are made beneficiaries. Exclusions or unexpected legacies (distributions of money) or bequests (non-monetary gifts) can cause emotional turmoil for survivors.

In most families, everyone knows pretty much what's likely to happen and a "no surprises" approach is often the best way to comfort survivors and maintain family coherence.

A will must state that the testator is of sound mind. It must be dated and must designate an executor who becomes responsible for making sure that the provisions of the will are properly executed and that the debts and taxes on the estate are paid. A will usually specifies a guardian for minor children. If the testator wishes to exclude a particular child, that child has to be named and left some amount, for example, one dollar, or else it can be argued that the child was forgotten.

When circumstances change after a will is prepared, for example, if a new child is born or if a specified property is sold and a new one acquired, a *codicil* can be added to modify an existing will. A will can be canceled or revoked if it's not rewritten after a divorce or if it's lost or destroyed. A new will should expressly revoke an old one. If it can be shown that the testator was unduly influenced by someone or was not of sound mind, the will can be invalidated.

When a person dies without a will, the person is said to die *intestate.* The court then appoints an administrator to distribute the estate according to the provisions of state laws, known as laws of intestate succession. Generally, this means that when there are no children, a spouse will inherit the entire estate. When there are children, a spouse inherits half of the estate and the other half is divided equally among all of the children. If there is no spouse but there are children, each child receives an equal share of the estate. If a person dies unmarried and has no children, first parents, then siblings, then grandparents, then aunts and uncles inherit the estate, in that order. Since only 40% of Americans have made a will, a court administrator will end up carrying out the inheritance laws for most families.

It can take months to probate an estate. The executor or administrator must prepare an inventory listing, valuing all assets of the estate, and identifying the debts and taxes that are owed. The executor must also ascertain the names of all of the potential beneficiaries and present them to the court. Known creditors have to be notified of the death, and an advertisement must be placed in the local paper to ensure that unknown creditors have an opportunity to present a claim. Normally, the executor is empowered to sell any of the assets in the estate to pay the bills. There are many ways to minimize the time and legal fees involved in a probate. Some people set up trusts that allow them to bypass probate. Others may place title to real property in "joint tenancy with the right of survivorship," so that the property automatically passes outside of probate to the survivor who is listed as the joint tenant, usually a spouse, a child, or a partner.

Most American families now have some type of life insurance as a part of their estate. Life insurance is especially useful for families if the breadwinner (or one of them) dies, because the money goes directly to the beneficiary rather than through probate and cannot be attached by creditors. Insurance proceeds are released immediately after a person dies and are not taxable. Many survivors may also be eligible for death benefits from Social Security, the Veterans Administration, and/or a union or employee benefit program.

Emotional Outcomes

Hidden in the dry details of the forms described in this chapter is the potential for significant emotional and social impact. Leanne, a retired Seattle police officer, has many stories about angry domestic disputes when police are dispatched to manage arguments about money and property after someone dies. She say all too often when someone dies, the police are called to settle family disputes. Often, they go out and break up a fight when one person in the family has taken charge of the estate without the consent of other members, or a fight erupts over a piece of property. Sometimes, family members don't believe that the documents being offered are legitimate.

Lenanne recalls a case where a man died 30 days before his mother. The dead man's sister brought in someone (who turned out to be an insurance agent), who persuaded the grandmother to sign a set of documents while she was extremely ill, leaving everything to a granddaughter. The sister also had her name put on the mother's bank account. When the family gathered, the sister announced that anyone who challenged the documents would be disinherited. The job of the police in such an instance is to calm everyone down and talk about sensible alternatives. In other cases, people enter a home where there is an aging relative and start stealing things, or they enter the home during the funeral and take things. There is no record of what was there. No one takes pictures of their possessions when they are dying, as they might for an insurance company. As Leanne points out, you can't prove what was there. She believes the best solution is to call the family together and let them know your wishes in person as well as in writing.

Long-term emotional fallout can occur in families when a member is cut out of a will or ends up disputing who gets what ring or set of dishes. Often these arguments reflect old family rivalries—such as an older sibling taking charge of the process and demanding to get first choice of property—evoking lifelong resentments about who was the favored child and who was forgotten. The sister of the deceased might claim that, before he died, her brother told her she could have his car, though he never mentioned this to his kids, who had hoped to sell it. The sister refuses to buy it from the kids because she considers it a gift from her dead brother.

Sometimes people believe that dying intestate solves any problems, because the estate will be distributed according to law; but laws don't keep people from arguing, feeling resentful, or getting their feelings hurt. State laws can also cause unexpected difficulties if they divide the estate equally between the spouse and the children. This means the surviving spouse may have to move out of the house and sell it in order to divide up the proceeds from the sale. For this reason, people of means set up joint tenancies that permit rights of survivorship for real property, bank accounts, and brokerage accounts. Rights of survivorship allow the spouse to receive assets without having to go through probate. Selling a house or another large asset may not only mean that everything needs to be split up, it may trigger excise taxes and other fees that diminish the estate, a loss that could have been avoided with proper planning.

Trusts, however, can come with their own emotional baggage. Grandma might leave her money in trust for her grandchildren, bypassing her son and daughter. When this happens, her adult children may have a hard time shaking the idea that she didn't respect the way they handled money or didn't trust their judgment as parents. Trusts are often created with age and purpose restrictions that make it seem as if Grandma is still trying to control everyone from the grave.

Taking the time to think about small bequests, such as a pair of diamond earrings or a big-screen TV, can help survivors avoid conflicts. When you make a will, most lawyers will ask if there are any valuable items or things that are so emotionally important that you want to specify who should receive them after you die. These are listed as "special bequests" in a will.

There are ways that families can handle splitting up an estate peaceably. Some families try to give each person a chance to name a few items among the estate's assets that he or she would like to have. Where there are several people who want the same things, these can be set aside and each person given another chance to choose from among the most wanted items. Horse trading can be encouraged, giving family members a chance to talk about why something was so meaningful to them. In this way, clearing up the estate can become a way to talk about the meaning of things, with the family meeting in a process of common grieving rather than on a battleground.

We know that families do better when they receive instructions about end-of-life matters from the deceased. That includes everything covered in this chapter, from whether and how to prolong life to funeral arrangements and the distribution of household goods. While it may be time consuming and even feel slightly macabre to think about these things in advance, in the end it will be a source of comfort for survivors, helping them realize how much you cared about them. It can help them to move on with their lives and appreciate the time you took in making clear arrangements. Most of us don't want our families to fall into disarray, arguing and being hurtful to each other over the few objects of significance we possess. The time you spend considering their feelings before you die can have a profound effect on your survivors.

References for This Chapter:

Legal Zoom. (2018). *What happens if you die without a will?* Retrieved from www.legalzoom.com/knowledge/last-will/topic/wills-intestate

PART THREE

What choices do we have now?

CHAPTER 8

LIVING WITH CHRONIC ILLNESS:
BETTER HEALTH THROUGH LIFESTYLE MEDICINE

According to medical researchers and many international health agencies, chronic diseases are an epidemic, having become the leading cause of death in the past few decades. A chronic condition is defined as a disease that lasts a year or longer and requires ongoing medical attention, potentially limiting one's daily life activities and reducing feelings of well-being. Ala Alwan, MD, former Assistant Director-General at the World Health Organization (WHO), classified chronic diseases as noncommunicable diseases, which include cardiovascular diseases, cancers, chronic respiratory diseases, and diabetes.

An alarming pattern of an escalating incidence of chronic diseases has appeared worldwide as lifestyle habits change and more and more people live long enough to join the ranks of the aging. Unfortunately, the world's healthcare systems were built primarily to treat infectious diseases and other acute conditions, not to take care of millions of people who suffer from long-term chronic illnesses. Today, chronic diseases are the world's biggest killers, responsible for an estimated 35 million deaths each year. That's 60% of all deaths globally. In the United States, as much as 76% of inpatient hospital care is now devoted to treating chronic conditions. This transition means that our current healthcare financing and operational orientation must shift emphasis from acute treatment toward preventative and ongoing care.

Among those over 65 in the United States, 85% suffer from one or two chronic diseases. Furthermore, nearly two-thirds of the people in this group are actually dealing with more than two chronic conditions. Even more burdensome for the healthcare system, chronic diseases are no longer isolated in the aging population. Among children under 17, nearly a quarter have one or more chronic diseases, and nearly half of adults aged 18 to 64 have one or more chronic illnesses, with 20% of this adult group coping with two or more such conditions.

Among children, respiratory diseases (such as asthma), eye disorders, and behavioral disorders are most prevalent. In the adult working-age population, hypertension, chronic mental issues, and arthritis predominate. The older you get, the more likely it is you'll have to cope with additional chronic conditions. Hypertension, heart disease, obesity, diabetes, eye disorders, and arthritis are most common. Dire predictions suggest that, by 2020, 164 million people, or almost half of the population, will have one or more chronic diseases and, more disturbingly, 81 million people in this group will have multiple chronic diseases.

The "demographic transition" of the baby boomers in the United States is the focus of grave concerns about the government's ability to care for people with multiple chronic diseases. Almost a fourth of all people in the United States will be 65 or older within the next 20 years. Boomers are typically arriving at the age of 65 with an average of one to three chronic illnesses that will plague them throughout their last phase of life. For some boomers, this means more than 30 years.

The projected numbers of affected boomers look foreboding. Today, 62% of the 8.6 million people aged 50 to 64 live with at least one of six common chronic conditions: diabetes; hypertension; high cholesterol; arthritis; heart disease; and cancer. Within the next 20 years, *six out of 10* boomers, or approximately 37 million people, will be managing more than one chronic condition. For example, one out of four boomers, or 14 million, will be living with diabetes, while 26 million, or approximately one out of every two, will live with arthritis. Over 21 million, or one out of three boomers, will be considered obese. This means that over 80% of our aging population will suffer from least one chronic disease that limits their well-being.

The prevalence of chronic diseases has created a crisis that is complex and multilayered. The healthcare system, and the citizens who must pay for it, will be faced with heavy increases in healthcare costs. In addition, families will need to manage the personal care of multiple generations, from aging parents to their children and, perhaps, grandchildren who are also plagued by chronic illness. This crisis will touch everyone at every age and, seemingly, all at once.

What Can We Do? (Or: Lifestyle Medicine)

A number of analysts have tried to explain the increased prevalence of chronic illnesses and have made suggestions for how to improve an increasingly overburdened healthcare system. Ultimately, however, the best solution starts at home with the willingness to learn how to better manage our own health. Many people are willing to accept the idea that they'll shorten their lives by a few months or years by smoking, eating poorly, and never quite getting around to exercise, but they don't often understand that dying prematurely is not the worst outcome. Having multiple chronic illnesses reduces one's quality of life significantly, decreasing mobility, activity level, and sense of well-being over long periods of time.

Research findings at the World Health Organization, Harvard Medical School, Kaiser Permanente, the World Cancer Research Fund International, and other important health and medical institutions have supported the argument that drugs and drug therapy are converting the fatal illnesses of the past into the life-long chronic conditions of the present. In other words, drugs may save and lengthen lives, but they do not resolve chronic diseases. Worse, the side effects of certain drugs too often add new long-term problems to an already growing list of chronic conditions. The question, then, is: What can we do in our daily life to prevent, lessen, or even reverse chronic conditions?

Dr. Alwan, former Assistant Director-General of WHO, has cautioned that if we fail to do something new, the disease burden on our global society will continue to increase. Indeed, the WHO and other health and medical institutions have begun to revolutionize the way they educate and promote healthcare practices. They are finding healthful ways for people to become less dependent on drugs and on extreme medical treatments and interventions. One of the clearest and simplest solutions they propose is eating a whole-food, plant-based diet.

There is evidence now that many, if not all, chronic conditions could be prevented by eliminating risky habits, such as tobacco use, and reducing the consumption of processed foods and alcohol. Increased physical activity has also been shown to be a big factor in controlling many chronic diseases. This is what many doctors and medical institutions term *lifestyle medicine*, and there is little doubt that dietary change is an essential part of the program they advocate.

Carmelo Mejia, MD, an Internal Medicine specialist at Kaiser Permanente in Oregon, puts it this way;

> As I see skyrocketing incidences [*sic.*] of conditions such as diabetes, hypertension, and heart disease, I am profoundly aware that there is so much potential for preventing or even reversing most of these problems through very inexpensive lifestyle changes centered on proper nutrition.

In light of the data they collected on lifestyle, Kaiser Permanente has decided to offer a "personalized, physician-led Healthy Living program" to combat chronic diseases. Physicians at Kaiser Permanente's Healthy Living program teach how to implement a whole-food, plant-based diet that can help people live a healthy life. The program follows the simple maxim that Michael Pollan teaches in his book, *In Defense of Food: An Eater's Manifesto*: "Eat food. Not too much. Mostly plants."

The Healthy Living program begins with an assessment that poses a few simple questions: Are you open to changing your diet if it could really improve your health? Do you want to lose weight? To feel better? To improve, stabilize, and even reverse a chronic condition such as heart disease, high cholesterol, diabetes, or high blood pressure? A "yes" to any of these questions leads to the next step: planning a whole-food, plant-based diet.

What is a whole-food, plant-based diet? It is a diet rich with plant foods that are eaten in their whole state, unprocessed and fresh. The idea is to eat each day a variety of vegetables, fruits, beans, lentils, seeds, whole grains, and nuts and small amounts of plant fats. Fortunately, there are many organizations that offer plenty of enticing menus and tasty recipes. For example, Forks over Knives (https://www.forksoverknives.com), the Center for Nutrition Studies (https://nutritionstudies.org), One Green Planet (http://www.onegreenplanet.org), Ornish Lifestyle Medicine (https://www.ornish.com), and many vegan magazines offer creative ideas for plant-based, whole-food meals with step-by-step instructions.

The whole-food, plant-based diet recommends eliminating animal products, such as meat, poultry, fish, dairy, and eggs. It also discourages processed foods, including oils and sugars. As alarming as that may sound to some of us, eliminating animal products and processed foods is only challenging in the beginning. Although it does take a commitment to our health and a willingness to change our views and habits, the results are truly worth the effort: feeling better; losing weight; and preventing, improving, or even reversing chronic conditions.

You don't have to do this all at once. You can start gradually eliminating meat and poultry. For example, you can set a target of five or fewer servings of meat per week and try switching to one of the nut milks for your morning cereal. For most people, this is a reasonably doable step that can make a big difference in how you feel and how your body functions.

The Politics of Health Research

Kaiser Permanente is not alone in their recommendations for how to combat chronic diseases with a whole-food, plant-based diet, but their program is actually quite courageous. Publicly endorsing whole-food, plant-based diets goes against years of commercial pressure by large animal factory-farms and food corporations to endorse meat, meat products (dairy and eggs), and processed foods. Some organizations, such as WHO and World Cancer Research Fund International have become quite politically active, urging governments around the world to change their health policies in hopes of stopping the current epidemic of chronic diseases.

WHO held its eighth global conference on Health Promotion in

Helsinki, Finland in 2013. In her opening address, Dr. Margaret Chan, Director-General of WHO at that time, called on nations to change their health policies, while praising Finland for their "health-in-all-policies" approach since 2006. Dr. Chan argued that demographic aging, rapid urbanization, and the globalization of unhealthy lifestyles are the reasons chronic diseases have now overtaken infectious diseases as the leading cause of morbidity, disability, and mortality all over the world.

General progress in living conditions and hygiene has led to vast improvements in controlling infectious diseases. These same improvements, however, together with great socioeconomic growth, have encouraged unhealthy lifestyles characterized by poor dietary habits. What propels these damaging dietary habits? Fats and sugars taste good! And we've been educated to think that meat and meat products are our best sources of protein. Indeed, the political origins of our poor dietary habits are interwoven with influential financial forces.

There is good evidence, according to WHO, that research findings about diet are ignored because of the business interests of powerful economic operators. Research has consistently demonstrated a strong link between chronic illnesses and certain foods and lifestyle habits such as smoking tobacco; not exercising; and eating meat, meat products, fats, sugars, and processed foods. Plant-based diets and healthy-lifestyle promotions are opposed not only by the tobacco companies, but also by "Big Food, Big Soda, and Big Alcohol." Unfortunately, the lobby power and immense wealth of the big food, drink, and animal-farming industries are not easy to overcome. Chan believes that these industries are not beyond funding scientific studies that confuse the evidence and keep the public in doubt.

Recently, the *New York Times* published an opinion piece by David Leonhardt claiming that Big Sugar has conducted misleading research about the effects of sweeteners, falsifying evidence on sugar's link to obesity, diabetes, and other effects. The *Times* piece was based on a large study from the University of California, San Francisco, and published in the *Annals of Internal Medicine*. Big Sugar is a good name for this industry as it has managed to include sugar in three-quarters of all packaged foods in American supermarkets, paying scientists to downplay the hazards of sugar in foods and drinks.

Researchers Brownell and Warner point out that we may have ignored good scientific research when the tobacco industry pressured and threatened, but we no longer can afford to ignore the data on the link between chronic illnesses and dietary habits. Fortunately, the film producer James Cameron has decided to produce a documentary film about the power of a plant-based diet featuring doctors, scientists, and world-class athletes. *The Game Changers* is both educational and motivating, showing us how athletes have adopted whole-food, plant-based diets, proving that meat is not necessary for protein, strength, and optimal health.

Let's Get Healthy

The WHO's healthy diet is similar to the recommendations of Kaiser Permanente, emphasizing plant-based whole foods while eliminating processed foods, sodas, sugars, fast foods, and meat products. The dietary guidelines of these leading medical organizations for plant-based whole foods are based on good scientific evidence. For example, Harvard's T.H. Chan School of Public Health published a study in 2016 highlighting the significant results that plant-based diets show in reducing the risk of type 2 diabetes. In January of 2018, Harvard Medical School published an article, "The right plant-based diet for you," that explains the many benefits of whole foods in a plant-based diet. Eating the whole fruit is much better than drinking 100% fruit juice because juices are high in sugar and do not include fiber. Here is a link to the WHO diet: http://www.who.int/news-room/fact-sheets/detail/healthy-diet

The scientific evidence on whole-food, plant-based diets is inspiring. Harvard Medical School published an article, "Becoming a Vegetarian," in the fall of 2017. The timing of the piece just before the winter holidays was not accidental, as that's a time many people overindulge in sugary foods, fatty foods, and alcohol. According to the American Dietetic Association, well-planned vegetarian diets (which include total vegetarian or vegan diets) provide "health benefits in the prevention and treatment of certain diseases." The Harvard Medical School team also reminded us that a healthy vegetarian diet is not filled with cheese pizza, sodas, and candy, which could technically be considered "vegetarian." This is one of the reasons that Kaiser Permanente has defined the vegetarian diet as whole foods that are plant-based, and emphasized the consumption of vegetables, fruits, beans, nuts, seeds, whole grains, and lentils.

Eating enough proteins is not as difficult in a vegetarian diet as some may think. Proteins are found in beans, whole grains, peas, lentils, seeds, nuts, and soy products. It is no longer considered important to mix grains and beans or other combinations of plants together in the same meal to create a full protein profile. Eating a healthy and varied diet of whole plants will naturally supply sufficient proteins and will usually make you feel fuller than animal protein because of the fiber contained in plants.

Eco-farmed and Organic Foods

Ecological and organic farming have also become a focus of research on health. Ecologically minded agricultural practices enhance the health of the planet and its inhabitants by using sustainable land-management systems that maintain biodiversity in food production. These practices include permaculture, biodynamic farming, local indigenous farming, wild harvesting, and organic farming. Eco-farming methods eliminate herbicides and pesticides, and do not use genetically modified seeds or plants.

The UN published a report in 2017 that estimated there are 200,000 acute-poisoning deaths from pesticides every year, with 99% of these deaths occurring in developing nations where environmental regulations are weaker. Long-term exposure to pesticides has been linked to various chronic diseases including cancer, Alzheimer's, and Parkinson's diseases; hormone disruption; and developmental disorders. What scientists find is that whole foods in their natural form, grown with ecologically sound agricultural methods, are best for both human health and the environment. A study led by Newcastle University showed that eating organic foods is associated not only with an increase of 69% in key antioxidants but also significantly lowered levels of heavy metals in organic crops when compared to crops grown conventionally with pesticides and other chemicals. The study concluded that a switch to eco-farmed or organic foods—especially whole, plant foods such as fruit, vegetables, beans, and grains—is beneficial to human and animal health.

Clean Home and Work Environments

Sick building syndrome is defined as a condition affecting office and factory workers, with symptoms such as headaches and respiratory problems. In 1991, revised EPA criteria differentiated between, on the one hand, symptoms of discomfort and acute-health problems that have no direct diagnoses and, on the other, diagnosable illnesses that can be attributed directly to airborne building contaminates. Almost a decade earlier, the WHO had suggested that up to 30% of new and remodeled buildings worldwide have unhealthy indoor air quality. Symptoms include eye, nose, or throat irritation, headaches, dry cough, itchy skin, fatigue, difficulty concentrating, sensitivity to odors, and dizziness and nausea. Although it had been thought that there is relief soon after leaving the building, scientists now believe that these inhaled chemicals can accumulate in the body.

Sick building syndrome is caused by a variety of factors from bad air ventilation, new carpeting, and manufactured wood products to those pesticides, paint, and cleaning agents that omit volatile organic compounds, including formaldehyde. Biological contaminants such as bacteria, molds, pollen, and viruses breed in the stagnant water found in humidifiers, drain pans, ducts, carpeting, or insulation. If a building is not ventilated well, pollution from outside sources, such as exhaust from motor vehicles or fumes from bathrooms and kitchens can enter the building. The same can be said for homes. Short of refitting buildings with green materials, there are a number of things that can be done to reduce the risks, according to the EPA. One simple approach is to open the windows. Air filters can be used to clean small spaces (a cubicle for instance). Spending a good 10 minutes outside a few times a day helps.

Most importantly, the EPA recommends that building occupants, management, and maintenance personnel fully communicate with one another to understand the causes and find solutions. Contact the EPA for more information on indoor air quality and sick building syndrome: https://www.epa.gov

The chemicals in the products we use in our daily life contribute significantly to both indoor and outdoor air pollution. A recent study on volatile organic compounds (VOCs) showed that industrial emissions together with consumer products—such as cleaning agents, personal care products, perfumes, air refreshers, pesticides, printing inks, and adhesives—contribute one-half of all the VOCs emitted in industrialized cities. Substituting these consumer products with chemical-free, biodegradable, and natural brands can have a great impact on the air we breathe at home and outside.

It is easier to make sure our homes are free of pollutants, chemicals, and molds than it is to do so in our offices. Replacing carpets with ecologically minded brands or wood and bamboo helps to keep chemicals such as formaldehyde and biological contaminants such as mold at a minimum. Steam cleaning, airing out the house, and vacuuming twice weekly is important to lower the mold, dust, and chemicals in old carpets. Initiate your changes one step at a time toward a better health. To learn more about creating a healthy home, check out the Environmental Working Group, EWG's healthy living home guide, at www.ewg.org.

Exercise and Meditation

You knew we'd get to this section sooner or later! Harvard Health considers exercise vital to health and well-being. In fact, aerobic exercise has been repeatedly demonstrated to fight several chronic diseases, while strengthening exercises protect our bones. Stretching eases backaches and keeps the joints lubricated. From walking, yoga, swimming, and jogging to light strength training, a variety of exercises have been found to offer the best anti-aging medicine. It doesn't have to be boring, either. Don't get stuck in a rut. You can alternate between different routines and times of the day, but keep it practical and doable.

There's also plenty of evidence that meditation is good for the mind and body. Many of us never stop to just relax our bodies, breathe deeply, and let our minds rest. Mind-calming meditations can lower the risk of heart disease, according to the *Journal of the American Heart Association*. Together with exercise, cessation of smoking, and observing a healthy plant-based diet, meditation is a key habit for a healthy lifestyle. Find a way to pause a nonstop, busy schedule and mediate. Even a short duration can enhance our ability to withstand stress and rekindle a sense of well-being.

Holistic or Natural Medicine

Many universities have integrative medical centers that offer holistic or natural medicine alongside the conventional approaches of allopathic medicine. For example, the physicians at Duke's Integrative Medicine clinic treat their patients with a holistic approach that takes into account physical, emotional, mental, social, spiritual, and environmental factors. Duke University endorses the WHO's definition of good health as "a state of complete physical, mental, and social well-being and not merely the absence of disease or infirmity." Alternative medicine and complementary medicine are modalities that focus on the whole person's well-being, using both natural and allopathic approaches. Each of these holistic models originated from the philosophical approach of naturopathic medicine.

At Kaiser Permanente, the Lifestyle Medicine clinic uses lifestyle medicine physicians and healthy living teams to assess and educate patients and implement healthy goals in their daily lives. Teamwork in medicine is not a new concept; however, integrating conventional methods of medical care with lifestyle changes is a holistic approach new to many conventional medical organizations. In fact, many medical centers now invite naturopathic doctors to join their teams. Integrative medicine combines philosophies from several schools of medicine and promotes innovative ideas on health and healing.

Combining science and natural medicine is important to living a healthy life. You can contact the different medical associations to find a naturopathic or integrative physician in your area, or ask your family doctor for such a recommendation. The most important step we can make in preventing chronic conditions is educating ourselves and mapping out a health plan. Start with a good whole-food, plant-based diet and a doable exercise program. Rid your home of chemical-laden products, substituting natural home and personal products. Ultimately our goal is to establish healthy life-style habits that will reverse or prevent chronic diseases.

References for This Chapter:

Anderson, G., & Horvath, J. (2004). The growing burden of chronic disease in America. *Public health reports, 119*(3), 263-270.

Corry, J., Wendel, B. (producers), & Fulkerson, L. (director). (2011). *Forks over knives*. [Motion picture]. United States: Virgil Films and Entertainment.

Leonhardt, D. (2018). Big Sugar versus your body. *The New York Times*, retrieved from, https://www.nytimes.com/2018/03/11/opinion/sugar-industry-health.html?emc=edit_th_180312&nl=todaysheadlines&nlid=493199200312

McDonald, B. C., de Gouw, J. A., Gilman, J. B., Jathar, S. H., Akherati, A., Cappa, C. D., ... & Cui, Y. Y. (2018). Volatile chemical products emerging as largest petrochemical source of urban organic emissions. *Science, 359*(6377), 760-764.

Pollan, M. (2009). *In defense of food: An eater's manifesto*. New York: Penguin Books.

Robert K., Pearlstein, E. (producers), & Robert K. (director). (2009). *Food, Inc.* [Motion picture]. United States: Magnolia Pictures.

CHAPTER 9

CHOOSING GOOD SUPPORT:
PALLIATIVE CARE AND HOSPICE SERVICES

In 2006, the National Quality Forum defined palliative care as:
> . . .patient- and family-centered care that optimizes quality
> of life by anticipating, preventing, and treating suffering.
> Palliative care throughout the continuum of illness involves
> addressing physical, intellectual, emotional, social, and
> spiritual needs and facilitating patient autonomy, access to
> information, and choice."

Palliative care is provided by healthcare workers at many levels, including basic care by a primary care physician or physician's assistant. It is also practiced by nurses, social workers, chaplains, pharmacists, and doctors that are board-certified in palliative care. The use of specialists has increased over the last few years and is expected to grow rapidly. Specialists are increasingly available outside of hospitals and hospices, in outpatient care, nursing facilities, and even at home.

The United States and other developed countries have developed palliative care partly because it allows people in the terminal phase of an illness to remain at home, and partly because it allows people to avoid unwanted tests and procedures. Terminally ill patients can stay home, remaining more comfortable and receiving better family support, outside the constraints of the more restrictive intensive care unit of a hospital. When you visit someone in the hospital (and especially in an ICU), it often feels strained and impersonal. It's hard to think about what to say in an environment that's focused on illness rather than on normal, everyday events. At home, conversation flows more naturally about the moment-to-moment activities of the day. Children and animals can hang around. Meals can be served when they're wanted rather than when they're scheduled, and no one needs to take your blood pressure in the middle of the night.

Palliative-care programs are also available in hospitals, which is especially helpful for patients with renal disease, neurological diseases, and heart failure. These units focus on pain, psychological issues, and the treatment of symptoms rather than on curative treatment. Palliative care begins with an assessment of the patient's physical needs, psychological symptoms, and care requirements. Healthcare professionals begin by assessing whether the patient understands the illness and the prognosis, with family members included in the discussion. Pain medication, antidepressant drugs, anxiety-preventing drugs, and social services that coordinate medical care, psychotherapy, and spiritual counseling may all be part of the plan. The family and the patient are all involved in creating a program that meets their needs, individually and as a collective, and honors end-of-life preferences.

Children and Palliative Care

Palliative care for children is built around the child's level of development. It offers pain management as well as therapeutic activities such as play therapy, music, art, and dance. It also provides support for parents and siblings and usually offers bereavement services. Collaboration, support, and empowerment are the themes for pediatric palliative care as outlined by the Committee on Hospice Care and the Institute for Patient- and Family-Centered Care.

Research shows that palliative care enhances the quality of life for patients and their families and reduces the use of costly emergency services and intensive care. It also encourages patients and families to use formal means, such as DNR orders, to express their preference for end-of-life matters.

A variety of palliative-care options are available in most communities. Eighty-five percent of hospitals with more than 300 beds offer palliative care. University hospitals are the most likely to have palliative-care units. Public and nonprofit hospitals are less likely to have them, and hospitals in the South have fewer such programs than elsewhere. Home-health services, however, offer palliative care, and many hospitals provide or coordinate palliative-care services in the home. Primary care physicians and oncologists may offer palliative care during office visits. Palliative-care programs are usually team-based and may involve a wide range of specialists beyond nurses and social workers. Diet, psychotherapy, occupational and physical therapy, as well as children's special services may be part of the package.

Because there is wide variation in the cost, quality, and management of palliative care, it is difficult to measure its impact. The available data, however, suggest that palliative care both lowers costs and raises the patient's quality of life. Such care is also associated with longer survival even when no curative treatment is received. It boosts the patient's chances of dying at home and decreases the number of hospitalizations.

One way to describe good palliative care appeared in the *Journal of the American Medical Association* in 2009. It's called the three Cs: competent; compassionate; and coordinated. High-quality palliative care is team-based, and includes family, friends, and professional help, from home-health assistance to spiritual support. Palliative care can be delivered early in the onset of a serious illness while curative treatments are still being evaluated. When setting treatment goals, good palliative care emphasizes taking time to communicate not just with patients, but with families as well. It recognizes that serious illnesses aren't just life threatening. They threaten the psychological, social, and spiritual well-being of the patient, the family, and the social network in which the whole family embedded.

Hospice Care

We addressed the hospice movement in Chapter 2. Like palliative care, hospice offers an alternative vision of dying that goes beyond pain- and symptom-management to promote patient autonomy, quality of life, and the opportunity to live life fully as long as possible. It assumes that dying patients can provide lessons in living.

As with palliative care, there is a large range of options to consider when choosing hospice care. There are for-profit, nonprofit, and government-run hospices. Volunteer hospices, like the one in Santa Barbara, do not provide palliative care directly, but offer volunteer companionship, the coordination of palliative care with other services, and free or low-fee psychological, social, and spiritual support. There are hospitals that offer hospice services and hospices that offer in-hospital service. There are also medical hospices that offer in-home support along with palliative care. Finally, there are standalone hospices that are actual physical facilities that allow patients to live out the end of their lives in a comfortable, caring environment, with palliative care and social services of all kinds.

The kinds of services available depend, in part, on how the hospice is funded. Free services are usually provided by organizations funded by endowments and grants. Most medical hospices are funded through Medicare and Medicaid and become available when a physician certifies that the patient is unlikely to live longer than six months. In these hospices, services may be provided for those without Medicare or other insurance, through endowments and grants.

Hospices that receive Medicare and Medicaid funds undergo careful evaluation of their services. They must provide nursing and physician care, medical social services, counseling, and volunteer services. Many employers help fund private insurance that covers part or all of the cost of hospice. To enter a hospice funded by Medicare means that one must refuse further curative treatment. This often makes it very difficult for families to accept a referral to hospice care. When there is confusion about whether a treatment that might prolong life should be considered curative, the hospice makes this decision. Patients must be recertified for hospice care every three months for the first six months. Medicare can continue to pay for hospice care beyond the initial six months if the patient's condition remains terminal, with recertifications every 60 days thereafter.

All hospices honor the patient's preferences for end-of-life care and offer a team approach that covers psychological, social, and spiritual needs in addition to medical care. They also support families in navigating Medicare and Medicaid forms, regulations, and requirements as well as the maze of private insurance companies. They may offer psychiatric services, physical therapy, occupational therapy, and even legal help, as well as funeral direction and coordination of other community resources.

Therapies using music, art, journaling, drama, dance—all forms of expression—may be supported by trained hospice volunteers, who also provide various other kinds of patient care. Volunteers can drive patients to appointments, carry out small housekeeping tasks, provide companionship, and support family members in coping with the dying process. Hospices usually also provide bereavement counseling and support for survivors.

In choosing a hospice-care provider, the range and quality of service are important considerations, along with support for the involvement of family and friends. But do they coordinate with community services, such as funeral direction, legal services, and local church and other civic-service groups? How well do the components of the multidisciplinary team communicate with each other? These things should be examined as well.

Large hospices are more likely to provide comprehensive services, and there are also geographic differences in the type of care they offer. As the 2015 Institute of Medicine report noted, it's very difficult to measure outcomes in end-of-life care across the many variations that exist. Patient and family satisfaction with palliative care and hospice care is most strongly related to communication with the family about the patient's condition. Regardless of whether or not the hospice was seen as providing the right amount of emotional support, a nurse was most often perceived by patients and families as playing an important role in the management and coordination of the patient's care. In a public opinion survey conducted in 2017, people noted that the professionals they trusted the most were nurses. This finding has remained steady in the poll over the last 15 years.

Researchers consistently find that hospice care is associated with lower costs, more services, and higher staff-to-patient ratios than hospitals. This is partly due, of course, to the fact that patients in hospice care must refuse expensive curative treatments and life-extending procedures. Since most patients are in hospice care for less than a month, it's hard to assess personal comfort or satisfaction. There are no adequate measures of psychological well-being or spiritual growth, and there is great variability in how much patients and family members are willing to say in any formal evaluation.

The Institute of Medicine identified 12 components of quality for end-of-life care, but the key component is whether care is flexible and tailored to the changing needs and desires of patients and families. Flexibility and tailoring necessitate frequent assessment, referral to palliative care or hospice as appropriate, and management of emotional distress. The Institute advocated direct contact between family, patient, and a specialist who is a palliative care physician, as well as round-the-clock coordination of care and services. Figure 8.1 presents the full list of components offered by the Institute with the rationale for the inclusion of each item.

The first decisions that must be made while sorting through all of these possibilities is whether the patient wants to die at home and whether the family is willing to and capable of providing home care. Because most people wish to die at home, it is critical to understand the benefits and costs of that preference.

Component	Rationale
Frequent assessment of patient's physical, emotional, social, and spiritual well-being	Interventions and assistance must be based on accurately identified needs.
Management of emotional distress	All clinicians should be able to identify distress and direct its initial and basic management.
Offer of referral to expert-level palliative care	Patients deserve access to specialist-level care when their needs cannot be met by non-specialist clinicians.
Offer of referral to hospice if the patient has a prognosis of six months or less	People who meet the hospice eligibility criteria deserve access to serviced designed to meet their end-of-life needs.
Management of care and direct contact with patient and family for complex situations by specialist-level palliative care physician	Care of people with serious illness may require specialist-level palliative care by a physician, and effective care by a physician requires direct examination and communication.
Round-the-clock access to coordinated care and services	Patients in advanced stages of illness require assistance with daily living, medication, physical comfort, and psychosocial needs.
Management of pain and other symptoms	All clinicians should be able to identify and direct the initial and basic management of pain and other symptoms.
Counseling of patient and family	Even patients who are not emotionally distressed face problems with loss of functioning, prognosis, finances, managing their symptoms, and family dynamics.
Family caregiver support	A focus on the family is part of the definition of palliative care; family members participate in care and require assistance themselves.
Attention to the patient's social context	Person-centered care requires awareness of the patients' social environment and needs for social support, including time of death.
Attention to the patient's spiritual and religious needs	End-of-life often has a spiritual and religious aspect and spiritual care is associated with quality of care.
Review and revision of care plan based on the changing needs of the patient	Care should fit current circumstances, which can mean that not all of the above components will be important or desirable in all cases.

Source: The Delivery of Person-Centered, Family-Oriented End-of-Life care.

Institute of Medicine, 2015.

Home Care

Given the choice, most people would prefer to die at home, if they can be pain-free, comfortable, and in control of their own lives. Families can choose hospice care at home if they want to keep a loved one out of a hospital or nursing home. Home care allows people to maintain relationships with family and friends, exercise choice, and generally feel more normal. For survivors, home care provides an opportunity for intimacy and a feeling that one is doing something meaningful for the patient, making a real difference in the quality of life for a loved one who is dying.

Home care can also be wearing. Today's caregiver must cope over long periods of time, given that life-extending treatments allow people with multiple chronic diseases to live longer. Smaller, modern families have fewer members to share the burden, so caregivers are less likely to have time to renew their own energy and revitalize their commitment. Home care is more complicated than it was for previous generations. There are often complex machines involved and complicated dietary and medicinal routines. Caregivers must coordinate in-home services, from visiting healthcare aides, nurses, and various therapeutic practitioners. Caregivers must see to daily bathing, toileting, dressing, and transporting the patient to appointments. Financial burdens become more onerous when caregivers must pay out-of-pocket costs and take time off from work. Family caregivers are seldom trained to deal with the emotional issues of a dying person and may have unmet emotional needs themselves.

Caregivers are encouraged to keep an open heart and practice deep listening. They are asked to be present emotionally while keeping up to date on all medical procedures and routines. Often, however, family caregivers are ignored by healthcare professionals or are denied access to information they could use to do a better job. Caregivers may let their own health and well-being go. They may not have time for their own psychological and social needs and can become ill and/or burned out without concrete support and physical help with the daily challenge of keeping the patient clean and comfortable. It's a tall order.

As the population ages and the elderly proportion of the total grows, pressure on families increases. Families often experience a sense of failure if they don't receive increasing levels of support as the patient's needs outdistance their ability to meet them. Nearly 70% of home-care patients receive no home visits from the physician. Over half of family caregivers will provide home-care for three or more years. The 2015 Institute of Medicine report estimated that, in 2009, the value of family caregiving hovered around $450 billion.

Families are likely to fall into "mutual pretense." Hoping to keep the patient from becoming too depressed, they avoid all talk about death or end-of-life decisions. Survivors fear such talk will cause the patient to give up the fight. Patients fear that bringing up the subject will drive people away. There is, however, scant evidence for either of these worries. No research has ever shown that accurate information about one's prognosis affects survival rates. And there's evidence that talking openly about dying can have a positive effect on adult survivors.

In 2015, the National Alliance for Caregiving published a report that characterized the typical family caregiver as a 49-year-old woman who cares for of a 69-year-old female relative. She provides at least 21 hours of care per week and earns $45,000 a year. She reports both emotional and financial stress, especially if she has to drive long distances or has trouble finding affordable food, transportation, and in-home help. She wishes she had respite care and more training in stress management. On average, she's provided care for more than three years and expects to continue for another five. Personal-care activities, such as dealing with incontinence, toileting, and showering, are the most difficult tasks that she faces, and she must often serve as an advocate and interact with medical personnel, providing them with important information about the patient's condition.

She's also likely to be involved in nursing care, from giving injections or tube feedings to catheter and colostomy care. She does all of this without any formal training, and she's likely to have no paid help and to feel that she has no choice but to be the caregiver. If she cares for a person with Alzheimer's, dementia, or other mental-health issues, she's likely to be particularly stressed. This caregiver feels she needs help in learning how to keep her patient safe at home, how to manage challenging behavior, and how to deal with issues around toileting. She is unlikely to ask for financial assistance or respite care, despite all of the strain.

Hospice and palliative care can alleviate stress and anxiety for both caregivers and the patients for whom they provide care. The mission of home hospice and palliative care is to put the empowerment of caregivers front and center. The needs and capacities of caregivers are assessed along with those of the patient; the focus of treatment is the patient/caregiver dyad. Caregivers receive training in nursing and in assistance in meeting the physical demands of caregiving. They also receive support in self-care, both emotional and social. Innovations in palliative care over the next few years should make it possible for home patients to receive curative and palliative care at the same time, allowing families more options and reducing the likelihood of repeated trips to the hospital and the doctor's office. Bridge programs are being devised to provide home-care support for patients who may not qualify for hospice because of an uncertain prognosis.

Research on caregivers is sparse and unsophisticated, but there are several new programs that focus on supporting them. Both respite and bereavement services are now covered under the Medicare hospice benefit. In all 50 states, Medicaid's Cash and Counseling program permits patients to pay family members small amounts for their services. Under the Program of Comprehensive Assistance to families, caregivers of seriously injured veterans may also receive stipends, training, and medical benefits.

Proper support for these programs will bring the benefits of home care to increasing numbers of patients and families, without the concomitant distress. According to the National Opinion Research Center (2014), 83% of caregivers, even under current conditions, report positive outcomes, including personal growth, having a meaningful purpose in life, the satisfaction of providing a high level of care, and a gratifying sense of giving back to someone who cared for them.

Caring for a dying person at home can bring unexpectedly intimate moments. Five years ago, Susan, a retired social worker, drove north from

Santa Barbara and arrived at the Monterey Airport in time to pick up her sister as soon as she arrived on her flight from Chicago. Their brother Steve had died at an early age. When they arrived at the house, her sister-in-law, Deb asked if we wanted to "see Steve." She led Susan and her sister upstairs and showed them where Steve was laid out right there in the bed where he died.

Deb told the two of them that, after Steve died, she spent the night sleeping with him in their bed. She said he was warm all night, and she felt comforted by his nearness. Susan felt both achingly sad, and overwhelmingly touched watching Deb struggle to relinquish custody of his body. She invited Susan and her sister to climb onto the covers with her and cuddle up while she told them about a woman she'd heard of who made memorial pottery vases out of clay mixed in with the ashes of the deceased. Then she asked Susan to trim Steve's hair so she could add it to the mix.

Finally, the three of them fell silent and just sat there together, surrounding Steve's body in their bed. It was an intimate and quite indescribable moment for Susan. Sensing that the pain had become too unbearable, Deb helped break the spell, when suddenly she suddenly blurted out, "My God, Steve, you stink!" And, Susan says, "It was true. He did."

A Good Death

In *A Common Sense Book of Death*, Edwin Shneidman described the dying person as alternating between acceptance and denial, a "hive" of emotions and sensations at the "coming and going" nexus of anguish, terror, distrust, pretense, taunting, and bewilderment. How, then, does one achieve a "good death"? Shneidman talks about a death that's compatible with the person's ideal sense of self and relatively free of conflict, one that permits continuity of relationships and the fulfillment of important wishes. In addition, mainstream culture emphasizes the importance of autonomy and choice, freedom from pain, and some semblance of well-being. Wouldn't dying with these principles intact be "good"?

The Institute of Medicine has defined a good death as one that's "free from avoidable distress and suffering for the patient, family, and caregivers, in general accord with patients' and families' wishes, and reasonably consistent with clinical, ethical, and cultural standards." One important piece of research, published in 2016 by the *American Journal of Geriatric Psychiatry*, reviewed 36 studies in which the researchers tried to define "dying well." The studies were drawn from articles published between 1996 and 2015. Participants ranged from 14 to 93 years of age and lived in 13 different countries including Asian, Middle Eastern, and European countries. The review article suggested that how we define a good death depends, to some extent, on the role we play. It examined this idea from the perspective of the patient, the family, and healthcare providers.

The authors identified 11 themes related to dying as an experience. The most frequently mentioned by all three types of participants was the importance of "preferences for a specific dying process." This construct referred to patients' being able to die where, how, and with whom they chose, and at particular time (for example, while sleeping). They also noted that dying well included having made appropriate arrangements, having signed advance directives, and having a plan for a funeral or memorial service. The second most frequently mentioned theme was "pain-free status," followed by "emotional well-being," which involved feeling at peace and in the absence of fear.

A secondary group of themes was mentioned in more than half of the studies reviewed. These included the opportunity to say goodbye, feeling that one's life has been well lived, and the ability to accept one's death. The idea of being respected and maintaining one's independence also appeared in the secondary themes, along with family support and preparation feeling that all treatment options had been exhausted, and a sense of control over treatment and end-of-life options.

There were some interesting differences among family participants, healthcare providers, and patients. Family members typically mentioned as important respecting patients' preference for the dying process and being pain-free, along with the feeling that the patient's life had been complete Among healthcare providers, patients' preference for the dying process was paramount, along with patients having their dignity, experiencing emotional well-being, and being pain-free. The importance of family and dignity was rated more highly by families than by patients, while patients reported that spirituality and religion were more important than families thought they were. Quality of life, however, was more important to families than it was not only to healthcare providers, but to patients as well. The authors concluded that families may be defining quality of life differently than patients. Despite these differences, all three stakeholder groups—patients, families, and healthcare providers—agreed that honoring the patient's preferences for dying was the most important constituent of a good death.

Taking a slightly different approach, other writers have emphasized what patients fear most: loss of autonomy; being unable to participate in enjoyable activities; loss of dignity and respect; and being a burden to others. The importance of emotional and spiritual well-being for patients suggests that team approaches should include both psychological and spiritual counseling.

The fact that patients, families, and healthcare providers all agree on the importance of patient preferences further highlights the emphasis we have placed on a deep and continuing conversation about those wishes. This includes not only a discussion about what the patient and the family want, but also frequent checks on how things are progressing in the light of those preferences. Talking about what constitutes a good death seems like a promising way to talk about end-of-life issues. What is a good death? One may be better for a warrior than for a sage, for a child than for an elderly person, for a person dying of cancer than for someone dying of emphysema. Without this conversation, there's really no way to know what a good death is for a unique person, in a specific family, working with a particular group of providers.

We sometimes talk about denial, surrender, and acceptance as the only alternatives. If we start, however, with the idea that people fear death because they're afraid it makes life meaningless, we can begin a conversation about how to make meaning from the experience of dying. Meaning is generally co-constructed in life. We make meaning out of things through talking with ourselves and with others. Denial shields us from the disquiet that drives dialogue to a deeper place, and perhaps acceptance and surrender do as well. If we can actually live with our dying, it may allow us to continue to co-construct the meaning of life with others, adding to our understanding of living what it means to be dying. Maybe we *can become* dying. That can be a lasting gift to others as we all struggle to understand what life and death are all about.

References for This Chapter:

Conner, S. (2009). *Hospice and palliative care: The essential guide* (2nd ed.). New York, NY: Routledge.

The Delivery of Person-Centered, Family-Oriented End-of-Life Care. Institute of Medicine. 2015. *Dying in America: Improving Quality and Honoring Individual Preferences Near the End of Life*. Washington, DC: The National Academies Press. doi: 10.17226/18748.

Williams-Murphy, M., & Murphy, K. (2011). *It's okay to die*. Retrieved from www.OKtoDie.com

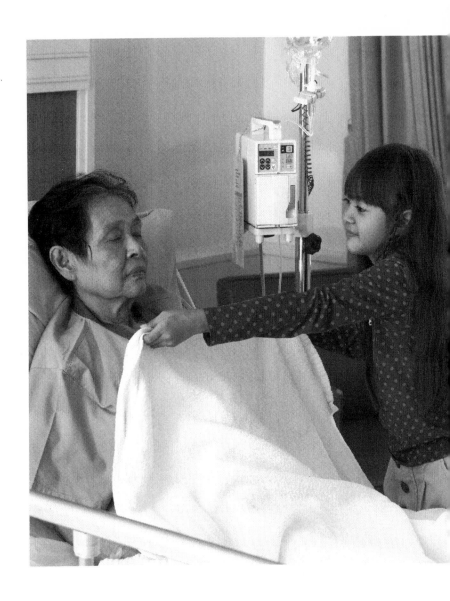

CHAPTER 10

FINDING THE RIGHT PLACE:
DYING AT HOME OR IN THE HOSPITAL

Everyone who is diagnosed with a terminal disease enters into one of four different trajectories. The first trajectory captures how most Americans would prefer to die: quickly and unforeseen. You're walking down the streets in good health when, suddenly, you keel over at a ripe old age. This preferred trajectory is hard on survivors, but easy for the deceased. Only about 10% of us will die quickly and without much warning.

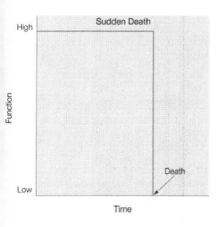 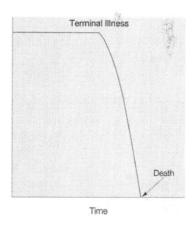

Source: Lunney, J.R. et al. (2003). "Patterns of functional decline at the end of life." *JAMA*.

Most of us will die of a chronic illness that will be treatable but not curable. Let's call this second trajectory a roller coaster.

There will be times when treatment improves our condition, and we feel better for a while, until the next crisis. After a hospitalization and more treatment, there's another reprieve, and so on. Some will have a shorter prognosis, like a quickly metastasizing cancer. Let's call this a short trajectory. Finally, some will leave more slowly but surely. Let's call this last one a slow trajectory:

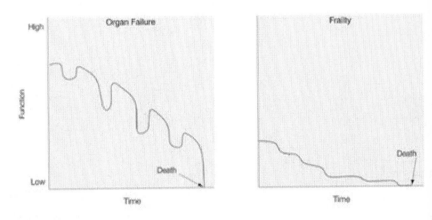

Source: Lunney, J.R. et al. (2003). "Patterns of decline at the end of life."
Journal of the Gerontological Society.

Dying in a Hospital

The 90% of us who experience one of the last three trajectories will most likely die in a hospital, in an intensive care unit (ICU) or in nursing care, possibly connected to IV drips and a feeding tube, a breathing tube, or both. Unless you have a Do Not Resuscitate (DNR) order in place, the doctor will attempt to resuscitate you and perhaps administer electric shock to start your heart beating if it stops. Cardiopulmonary resuscitation (CPR) is unlikely to be successful, however. Currently, 92% of Americans who go into cardiac arrest remain dead. Of those who are resuscitated, over half will have suffered irreversible brain damage. The longer it takes to revive you, the more likely it is that you'll never be yourself again, especially if you're elderly and in poor health.

This isn't to say that CPR is never a good idea. A healthy 50-year-old man who suffers cardiac arrest will probably want doctors to do whatever it takes to bring him back. A woman with a terminal illness or one who's 95 and has little energy left for life may well choose to file a DNR order. That's why you should review your advance directives whenever circumstances change.

If you're experiencing a roller coaster trajectory with its frequent crises, you may easily end up in the ER or a hospital bed. There you must either receive curative treatments, be taken home, or transferred to a nursing-care facility. Once you're in the hospital, medical rules, regulations, and standardization drive your daily routine. Your family may need to observe visiting hours and leave the room whenever there's a change in your status. There's little room for intimacy and heartfelt conversation when at all hours of the day and night there are machines buzzing and clanking, the staff are coming and going, and on the other side of the curtain there's another patient.

If you enter the hospital through the ER, your family may not be allowed to stay with you, even though research suggests that most family members who witness a resuscitation attempt find that it relieves their anxiety. On the other hand, some people find that watching a resuscitation attempt only leaves them with traumatic memories. In the ICU or during any stay in the hospital, pain control is usually poor, and the patient's wishes can be lost in the confusion. If you survive the hospital stay and can't be cared for at home, you'll probably enter a nursing facility. This is also true if you refuse treatment in the hospital. Nearly a third of all terminally ill patients die in nursing homes. These days, however, many nursing homes offer hospice and palliative care.

Hospital-based physicians and nurses are seldom trained to deal with death, and many report high levels of death anxiety. Older doctors and nurses and those who specialize in fields like gerontology and oncology, however, show lower levels of death anxiety, which may explain their choice of specialty in the first place. Monica Williams-Murphy, an oncologist who wrote "It's Okay to Die" with Kristin Murphy, has claimed that the only training she ever received about death was when she was told that if she informed a family of a patient's demise, she should be sure to use the word "dead."

According to the National Academy of Science, the quality of communication between clinicians and patients who are nearing death falls short, especially when discussing prognoses or emotional and spiritual issues. Most people near the end of life are not in good enough cognitive or emotional condition to make their own decisions about medical care. In fact, 70% of the elderly are unable to make decisions as they approach death; they will, almost certainly, receive full emergency care, including resuscitation, from physicians who don't know them. Conversations with family and physicians about end-of-life preferences, with an even greater detail than advance directives, are needed to ensure that patients' preferences are honored. Unfortunately, even people who've been diagnosed with terminal diseases are unlikely to have these conversations until they are critically ill. Admission to the ER or the ICU is probably the worst time to initiate a dialog about preferences around dying.

Mental health issues such as depression and anxiety often dominate discussions with patients who have the kind of chronic illnesses that require intermittent hospitalization. Patients in acute crises are unlikely to talk about their preferences, and doctors aren't good at guessing what they might be. For that matter, in the absence of advance directives or end-of-life conversations, neither are family members. Of course, the situation is even worse when patients exhibit dementia. Alzheimer's disease was the sixth leading cause of death in the U.S. in 2013, according to the Centers for Disease Control. Nearly one-half of Americans over 85 have this disease and, of that number, only half are able to make their own decisions. In addition, many families don't understand that dementias are progressive. As a result they're likely to request CPR when a patient can no longer decide for themselves.

A part of this problem can be attributed to the poor communication skills of physicians, who often avoid discussing end of life and speak in ways that are overly optimistic. In one study of nearly 200 doctors caring for patients who died in a hospital, only 11% reported speaking about death with any patient. Formal training in advance directives is rare in medical schools. It's usually the case that even when palliative-care physicians are brought in as consultants, they never actually talk to the patient. Less than .08% of physicians are certified in palliative care, making it difficult for them to meet face-to-face with the many patients they may treat.

One source of help that's often overlooked in hospitals is chaplaincy. Chaplains are certified by the Association of Professional Chaplains. They must have an undergraduate degree, a letter of endorsement from a recognized faith, and 2,000 hours of experience, along with certain courses in a graduate theology program and a clinical pastoral education. Use of a chaplain is associated with lower rates of hospital mortality and higher rates of hospice enrollment. Chaplain services can be very helpful when dealing with a patient who is nearing death, whether or not a family is religious. In contrast to doctors, most chaplains don't fear death and are trained to deal with family distress in a calm, grounded manner.

Financial Costs and Incentives

Dying in the hospital can be a huge financial burden, even for Medicare patients or patients with private insurance, unless they have supplemental-care insurance. Without a supplement, patients must bear 20% of the costs themselves. ERs and ICUs are expensive, as are transitions across settings (e.g., from the hospital to a nursing facility). The American system of healthcare insurance pays for expensive therapies and procedures, but it offers little support for families who are trying to keep a dying patient at home and need help with dressing, bathing, and feeding. Many dying patients place enormous physical demands on their caregivers and may also exhibit psychological problems that are difficult to manage. When they can't afford help, distressed caretakers end up taking the patient to the hospital, where they risk unsolicited treatments and procedures and an unwanted transfer to a nursing facility. Of course, these strategies also trigger large deductibles and co-pays.

Medicare and Medicaid services pose a challenge to the nation's fiscal health. They consume an ever-growing proportion of public spending, limiting investments that may impact the health of the entire population, such as education, housing, infrastructure, and the environment. Both Medicare and Medicaid expenses are expected to increase substantially over the next 10 to 15 years, as baby boomers living with multiple chronic illnesses move into old age. The proportion of taxpayers who pay for Medicare and Medicaid will also decline over that same period. Moreover, the cost of treatments, procedures, and medications in the U.S. is higher than in other countries, accounting for over 90% of the increase in prices for healthcare during the first decade of the twenty-first century. Though there's debate about whether these prices will continue to escalate, there's little doubt that the expansion of community and social services would help to contain costs. Poor coordination among different components of the healthcare system makes it difficult for patients, families, and administrators to know whom to contact for approval of services or which agency to bill, adding to everyone's stress and creating a greater reliance on emergency care.

Fee for Service

The 2015 Institute of Medicine report stated that fee-for-service payments give rise to perverse incentives that encourage doctors to order unnecessary tests, procedures, and hospitalization. The fee-for-service payment system also discourages referrals to hospice and palliative care. More than 40% of late enrollments in hospice are preceded by an admission to the ICU. In 2009, one study reported that, although 42% of Medicare patients who died were enrolled in hospice care, nearly 30% were in hospice for only three days or less. Hospitals encourage the transfer of dying patients to nursing facilities. Infections, falls, and medication errors increase during these transitions, not to mention the patient's discomfort and disorientation. Half of all of Americans visit the ER in the last month of their lives. Three-quarters do so in their last six months. These visits usually result in hospitalization.

One part of the problem lies in the fact that many dying patients either don't understand or haven't been clearly informed that they're dying and that there's no effective treatment for their condition. These patients are often unaware of alternatives such as palliative care or hospice. The fee-for-service system doesn't reimburse the cost of the coordination, management, and evaluation services that help patients understand their disease, explore their treatment options, and establish a plan of care. Our healthcare-finance system also limits or caps the ancillary services that improve patient mobility, communication, and self-care. Clearly, investment in these services might reduce the number of ER admissions.

The operations of nursing-care facilities are also based on some strange incentives. Patients who can't be cared for at home usually enter skilled-nursing care when they're discharged from the hospital. Nursing homes are well paid by insurance companies for treatment and procedures if a patient is in crisis, but they're poorly paid for long-term, non-acute care. Repeated transfers from nursing care to the hospital are common because hospital patients are initially sent to nursing homes while still in need of acute care. This is especially true of patients with dementia. If they can be hospitalized for reasons other than their dementia, they can return for acute care in the nursing home, allowing it to bill at the more generous rate. Transfers like this are expensive and burdensome for patients and families. Here, long-term care insurance can be very helpful, but it's also expensive for older people. This constitutes an excellent reason to explore long-term care when you're still young and healthy and to start thinking about end-of-life choices early in adulthood.

In 2013, the U.S. Senate Commission on Long-Term Care proposed a shift from nursing to home care as a focus of funding, but the shift has been complicated by poor communication between medical services and community resources. Families end up trying to cope with a mix of federal, state, and local resources that have different caps, procedures, and rules. One solution that's been tried is community-based, palliative-care services that can provide the management and coordination these families need.

Many patients are seen in several settings and interact with several physicians. They experience multiple handoffs and are offered a variety of treatments and medications that interact with each other in unfortunate and sometimes unknown ways. Better coordination is often seen as the key to better end-of-life care. Studies designed to assess the effectiveness of coordinating care have reported that, if patients receive expert care coordination, they're more likely to follow treatment guidelines and adhere to medication regimes and less likely to be hospitalized and use unnecessary medications.

Prolonging Life

A hospital may not be the optimal place to die, but it's often the best place to receive treatment and procedures that may prolong your life. When is that a good choice? It seems pretty obvious that healthy people who, for example, have suffered a cardiac arrest, are in a coma, or have been badly injured might want doctors to use every means at hand to prolong their lives. A healthy person may want to create advance directives that express a preference to die in the event of brain death but otherwise receive resuscitation, even when the chances of success are slim.

We've talked quite a bit about DNRs and refusing heroic measures. If you're dying, however, you have the right to request a "full code," which means that your doctors and nurses will do everything possible to save you. This may range from CPR to the use of a heart-lung machine or even experimental treatments. A variety of legal and ethical issues, however, have been raised about this choice. Some writers have pointed to consequences, aside from the discomfort of broken ribs or the risk of waking up with brain damage, that argue against using every possible means to resuscitate a person. The administration of futile measures at the end of a person's life consumes resources that might best be deployed for others who are likely to survive. In other words, *triage* or rationing— the sorting of patients to determine an allocation of treatment, according to a system of priorities that maximizes the number of survivors—may best serve the common good.

Courts in the U.S. have come down on the side of patient choice rather than triage. A person who is considered mentally competent has a right to choose any available treatment for their condition. For example, courts have decided that a dying person has the right to choose an experimental drug before it has been proven in *randomized trials*, regardless of the doctor's opinion about the probability of success. Randomized pharmacological trials are experiments in which some patients are given a drug which has not yet been proven effective, while others are given a placebo (a pill with no pharmacological effects), in order to test whether or not the new drug is effective. Today, if patients are competent, they may choose freely, regardless of the cost. But some ethicists believe that giving patients the right to choose is contrary to the greater good because it causes dying patients to shy away from randomized trials where they might receive a placebo. When patients refuse randomized trials, it becomes difficult to test a drug properly, potentially compromising the best interests of the public. The rest of us bear the cost of allowing patients to make such decisions against the best judgment of their physicians.

Another argument, most often posed by physicians, is that patients who choose to prolong life don't really know what they're getting into. They don't appreciate the suffering or the risks involved in *intubation*, the surgical installation of a tube down their trachea so they can breathe or of a feeding tube into the stomach. In their decision-making process, patients tend to minimize the side effects of ever more powerful drugs or of procedures such as total brain irradiation. Whole-brain radiation, for example, induces neurological deterioration and dementia in up to 90% of adults over 60, resulting in side effects that can include problems in walking and urinary incontinence.

In *Die Wise* (2015), Stephen Jenkinson objected to the belief some people have that if you *can* live you *should*, until all the wealth, sanity, and caring is exhausted. These patients refuse to stop treatment, even if the situation is futile. They feel the need to do something—anything. Jenkinson also contended that palliative care is not the answer. Palliative care gives people time that they don't know how to enjoy. Dying people, in Jenkinson's view, choose life-extending procedures and palliative care because they're terrified of dying. But more time won't solve that problem. It will just result in more days of fear and suffering at the end of life. More time doesn't restore the person to health; it only prolongs dying, engendering more drug use, more side effects, and more dependence. Nor, Jenkinson argues, does it help families who, for months and sometimes years, must live without knowing how to move forward. The dying person's continued living has become the problem. The fear of dying can cast a shadow over every waking moment, eventually fueling the demand for physician-assisted suicide.

Similarly, in *Being Mortal*, Atul Gawande, a surgeon and professor at Harvard, claimed that doctors have too long seen their job as ensuring health rather than well-being. He argued that medicine too often inflicts unnecessary suffering on the dying by recommending ever more aggressive treatments, with their increasingly debilitating side effects, to people who are already dying. Doctors do this without an honest discussion of what patients' lives will look like if they survive for a few more weeks or months. According to Gawande, our experiment in making mortality a medical experience has failed.

Finally, in *It's Okay to Die*, Monica Williams-Murphy and Kristin Murphy maintained that we need to embrace natural death and place our focus on making the end of our lives as free from suffering as we can. In their view, we should reduce the number of costly, unwanted treatments that may or may not offer a few more days, weeks, or months, and use the savings to support hospice and home care. We should create a "high touch/low tech" model that allows one to live out their days with dignity, pain-free, and surrounded by those who love them.

If you prepare advance directives for yourself, you have the opportunity to create the kind of dying that reflects your needs, capacities, and resources and those of your family. But there are many options, and the consequences of each option must be explored. You should know, for instance, that a feeding tube is passed into the nose, down the esophagus, and into the stomach. It can cause nose pain and sinus infections and is easily displaced; sometimes it's mistakenly pushed into the lungs. For longer-term feeding, the tube must be inserted through one's skin directly into the stomach or intestine. Bleeding, infection, and accidental perforations of other organs are not uncommon. Tracheal intubation is a procedure designed to allow the patient to breathe more easily. A tube is placed in the airway and attached to a breathing machine. Breathing this way makes it difficult to communicate and is quite uncomfortable. It automatically triggers admission to an ICU for care. And its insertion can accidently induce regurgitation, aspiration of the vomitus into the lungs, and a wicked bout with pneumonia.

As we've shown, it is increasingly important to know what you're getting into when you face end-of-life choices. There are long lists of interventions—with benefits and side effects—that can be deployed to prolong life. Few of them are free of problems, and none can guarantee a substantial increase in either the longevity or the quality of life for a person who's nearing death. So how do you decide? As Williams-Murphy and Murphy have suggested, there's no need for anyone who's dying to suffer from pain. It seems to us that many interventions that prolong life for a short period not only do little to make dying easier, they can create substantial barriers to communication, family care, dignity, and the opportunity to grow and develop up to the very end of life. In the next chapter, we explore some of the signs that one is reaching the end and some of the phenomena that people experience in their last few days and weeks. Being alive to the possibilities inherent in every last minute of life may be preferable to extending a hospital-centered existence, hooked up to tubes and confined to a bed.

References for This Chapter:

Gawande, A. (2014). *Being mortal: Medicine and what matters in the end.* New York, NY: Metropolitan Books, Henry Holt and Company.

Jenkinson, S., & Shaw, M. (2015). *Die wise: A manifesto for sanity and soul.* Berkeley, CA: North Atlantic Books.

Williams-Murphy, M., & Murphy, K. (2011). *It's okay to die.* Published by the authors and MKN, LLC. For information email infor@OKto-Die.com

CHAPTER 11

WHEN THE END IS NEAR: BODY, MIND, AND SPIRIT

Because people live so long in the U.S. and because so many people develop multiple illnesses, there is, just before a person dies, a *liminal phase* between life and death that may last a few days or weeks. Liminal refers to a threshold point as the dying person approaches what we might call the "last door." There is little wisdom about this experience and few customs, rites, or rituals to guide our behavior. Writers from Martin Heidegger to Kübler-Ross have described the possibility of continuing to be present during this phase and of becoming more appreciative of the everyday beauty of life, drawing meaning from the events you have experienced, and focusing on what is essential. In this chapter, we explore the signs, symptoms, and challenges of the liminal phase.

In the postmodern world, medicine allows us greater control over the manner of our death. We don't have to live with relentless pain, and we have better opportunities now than 10 or 20 years ago to die in a place of our choosing, with the people we love around us. We're free to choose a natural death and refuse life-sustaining treatments. Or we can request that our lives be maintained as long as possible. Most of us will live long enough that our deaths won't be considered premature, and most of us will die of chronic illnesses. Our deaths won't be unexpected. Two-thirds of Americans make it through their sixty-fifth birthday and half of those who die after 65 will be in reasonably good health until the last few months.

Body Processes

As death approaches, there are a number of signs and symptoms. Dying people are often aware of these indicators. Many people have premonitions about their own death for as long as a year in advance. While we don't know exactly what triggers these premonitions, we do know that cognitive changes can be observed in dying people two or three years before they actually die. There's also a progressive loss of energy that becomes more pronounced as a person succumbs to a chronic illness.

Dying people begin to sleep more and feel increasingly weak during the last months of life. Often, they visit a doctor to see if something more can be done or if something new has gone wrong. As fatigue and muscle weakness increase, mobility declines, until one isn't able to walk much any more. A wheelchair or walker becomes essential along with a hospital bed that allows for different positions. They may eventually become bedridden. People in the terminal stage often fall and then have difficulty recovering from any injuries. A broken hip can put a dying person in the hospital. The broken hip may be addressed, but limited mobility in the hospital or, afterward, at home can lead to a pneumonia that won't respond to treatment.

In the final weeks, a palliative-care provider may recommend stronger medication. Eventually, a sedative may be required to protect the person from pain and discomfort. Dying people also lose their interest in food and feel nauseous much of the time. They may need to start using nutritional supplements or an appetite stimulant. At some point, they may quit eating and drinking entirely, motivating families to call 911. The EMTs come and take the patient to a hospital to be hydrated with IV fluids, fed temporarily through a tube, or given oxygen. Dying people can become agitated, restless, or confused, especially in the evening. They might become increasingly detached from their environments and from people around them. They may appear to be unable to think or make decisions and may eventually stop trying to communicate at all.

Swelling of the extremities is common in the final days, as well as complaints about shortness of breath. Sometimes, a diuretic can alleviate the swelling, and an oxygen mask can provide some comfort. In a hospital a machine can assist breathing by forcing air into the lungs. Heart rate can become very rapid—or slow down. Blood pressure may drop precipitously or shoot up to dangerous levels.

Patients who are dying of cancer experience fever, chills, and sweating as their immune system continues to decline and the cancer spreads. They're likely to develop infections and to have allergic reactions to various drugs. Often, the immediate cause of death is an infection accompanied by fever and pneumonia. Those who die from heart disease or lung failure will likely experience a series of attacks followed by periods of recovery, despite overall declines in health. This is the roller coaster trajectory that was depicted in Chapter 10.

Death from cardiac arrest can appear to be sudden, but it's often the result of a gradual deterioration over a period of months or years. Those who die of dementia or stroke are most likely to enter the terminal phase in very poor health and experience a gradual decline that reflects the failure of multiple functions. Many suffer a series of small strokes that can look more like the roller coaster typical of heart and lung disease. Of course, massive stroke or heart attack can unexpectedly cause a sudden death as well.

Active dying, in the last few days, is usually accompanied by social withdrawal, irregular breathing, disorientation, and agitation. Dying people may twitch, pick at their bedcovers, try to climb out of bed, or pull off tubes and breathing apparatus. These symptoms can be quite distressing for families, but they're a normal part of active dying. Increased sleeping and decreased consciousness are also normal, along with changes in skin color and temperature. As death draws near, the skin becomes pale, even bluish, and is cool to the touch.

At the moment of death, the muscles relax. As throat muscles give way, the person may emit a death rattle as they exhale. Bowel and bladder muscles fail. The heart usually beats for a few minutes after the person stops breathing, and a brief shudder or seizure occurs. The jaw falls open, and the eyes become locked in a fixed stare. Finally, the person can no longer be aroused, and is pronounced dead.

Psychological Experiences

In the days and weeks before death, patients, families, and those who are helping them report deathbed visions and odd coincidences that happen with such frequency that they should be considered normal. The Shared Crossing Project (www.Sharedcrossing.com) offers a chart on its website presenting various phenomena associated with the end of life, including pre-death premonitions, dreams, and visions. It also includes post-death experiences among survivors and those who've had near-death experiences or shared-death experiences. The graphic below illustrates the spectrum.

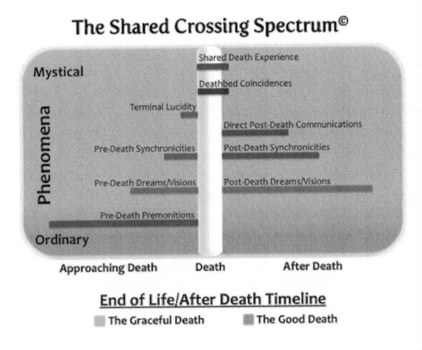

Source: Shared Crossing Project at www.SharedCrossing.com

In 2016, *Psychology Today* published a two-part article on *deathbed visions* written by Marilyn Mendoza, a clinical instructor in psychiatry at Tulane University. A deathbed vision is one of the experiences a dying person may describe in the days or weeks before death. These visions usually include seeing beautiful scenery or a dead family member or religious figure. Mendoza reported that nearly 60% of these visions involve dead relatives—often a mother, father, husband, or wife—who come to take the patient to the other side.

Sometimes these visions include a deceased pet. Most often the relative that appears is the mother, although people often see angels or a religious figure such as Jesus. We have no idea why or how these visions happen, though scientists usually treat them as hallucinations. Deathbed visions can be quite vivid. There may be brilliantly colored trees and flowers, bright lights that seem to beckon to the patient, or beautiful music. Often patients stare into a corner of the room as if viewing an invisible tableau. They may reach out and appear to hug someone or have a silent conversation. Regardless of the explanation, patients and healthcare providers consistently report that such visions relieve the anxiety of patients and those around them. Dying people are comforted by these experiences and often lose their fear of death afterward. You can find more information about them at: https://www.psychologytoday.com/us/search/site/deathbed%20visions.

In 1977, Karlis Osis published a book called *The Power of Death*. Based on thousands of reports and interviews with hundreds of doctors and nurses, he concluded that dying people find great comfort and happiness in these experiences, as well as relief from pain and a sense of peace. Osis believed that such experiences shouldn't be called hallucinations, as patients continued to have good awareness of their real surroundings. In addition, he found no difference in the frequency of the visions between patients who were religious and those who were not.

Given that only about 10% of patients are conscious in the hours before their deaths, we don't know how many dying people have these experiences. But of the people who are conscious, more than half seem to have them. On rare occasions, these visions are shared by friends or relatives who are present. The Shared Crossing Project calls this a *shared death experience* and focuses on helping people learn how to attend to such an experience in a supportive way rather than dismissing it as a hallucination.

We discuss *near-death experiences* (NDEs) in the next chapter.

NDEs take place after a person is dead. Deathbed visions occur before a person's death and generally include only figures of people that are already dead or symbolic figures such as angels. In fact, many accounts describe a vision of a dead relative who had died so recently the patient didn't know the person was dead. Sometimes these visions are accompanied by unexpected lucidity. After hours in a coma, patients open their eyes just before dying and reach out or sit up, stare at the corner of the room, and smile.

The Division of Perceptual Studies at the University of Virginia School of Medicine has also been studying a phenomenon they call *crisis apparitions*, in which people see a lifelike image of a person who is dying or who is involved in an accident, at a time when they have no normal way of knowing that the event has taken place. These apparitions appear sometimes to people who are awake and sometimes during dreams, or they may simply present as an odd physical or emotional sensation that coincides with the event. One of the authors had such an experience, Dohrea writes:

On a flight to Chicago, I started thinking about my father, who lives a half a world away. It was time for me to call him for one of our typical long chats. But memories kept bubbling up more and more vividly, to the point of hearing my father speak to me softly in Hebrew with his sweet Romanian accent. I was, to say the least, quite surprised. I have heard of deathbed visions shared by family members, yet the thought he was dying did not enter my mind. It was so good hearing his voice!

My father has always been one of my best friends, so I welcomed this unexpected experience and for hours I felt his presence and heard him gently share his joys and worries. As I traveled, my father seemed to sit right next to me, reminiscing, and asking me to check up on certain family members. He simply joined me while I handled the usual details of traveling by air and car. At the hotel, all of a sudden, I lost contact with him. The next morning my mother

phoned. My father [had] died several hours after an emergency surgery, the exact time he spent with me. For years
my father told me how much he relied on my steadfastness
and clear mind. His extraordinary visit may have sprung
from my own imagination, yet my father's presence and
love felt real. More research on deathbed visions and vis-
itations is needed to further understand these experiences.

The website for this research acknowledges the sparseness of systematic data on experiences such as these, but what research there is suggests
that such visions are common and may not be hallucinations related to drugs
or particular illnesses. In fact, drugs and fevers can actually suppress these
experiences rather than generate them. You can find out more about these
experiences at: www.med.virginia.edu/perceptualstudies/types-of-cases.

In a study of hospice patients in Buffalo, New York, researchers
have reported that nearly all of the patients had near-death dreams or visions. These events usually offered patients opportunities to engage with
deceased family members or to see loved ones who were "waiting" on the
other side. In these dreams and visions, people often reported feeling reas-
sured that they'd been good parents, children, or workers. The researchers
in Buffalo argued that these experiences were not products of delirium. The
visions were not confused or disorganized, and when patients shared them,
as they often felt compelled to, their stories were coherent and comforting.
These researchers encourage families to see this type of experience as both
a normal part of the dying process and, if family members aren't fearful, a
chance to meaningfully engage the patient.

About one in five of such visions is distressing. This usually occurs
when patients revisit traumatic events such as a war or a natural disaster, as
if trying to resolve or integrate it. There are disagreements about how these
negative experiences should be treated. Some doctors recommend anti-anx-
iety or antipsychotic drugs, while other care providers believe they should
not interfere, even if the patient is distressed. Several writers have proposed
that these experiences may be unconscious attempts to work through earlier

trauma. The Buffalo researchers argued that these experiences signify a attempt to come to terms with life events from the past and to find meaning

Patients, family, and clinicians report a reluctance to engage the pa tient's experience because they feared either the dismissal of these events o even being ridiculed by medical caregivers. The Buffalo researchers argue that these dreams and visions present an important therapeutic opportunit for clinicians to support patients and families in the transition from life t death. They believe that these experiences can relieve anxiety and ease suf fering, bringing comfort and some closure. There would seem to be littl reason not to engage these experiences, as long as one feels curious an unafraid.

End-of-life Rituals

In Dying with Confidence, Anyen Rinpoche wrote about dying from the Buddhist perspective, encouraging those who are dying to reflect o their lives and on their death. He believes that reflections on one's dying ca serve as a spiritual practice, allowing people to continue developing throug the end of life. For devout Buddhists, who've been preparing for death mos of their lives, dying is the best opportunity for enlightenment; one needs t make good use of it.

In his book, Rinpoche outlined three stages of the liminal phase o life that can enrich this reflective practice. First, the dissolution of the sense occurs. There's a loss of hearing and then of vision, and then taste, sme and, finally, touch. In this first phase, friends and family should encourag the person to stay conscious through mindfulness practice. The next phas is the dissolution of the elements, beginning with the sensation that one i extremely heavy or falling into a hole and concluding with the water in th body being affected; one becomes thirsty. Then comes a phase, which h referred to as *the fire*, leading to the loss of one's ability to speak and, even tually, to a cessation of the inner breath.

Rinpoche teaches that pain medication can be very useful in thi process, as long as one remains conscious. Pain medication can help peopl to focus and to remain calm and stable. The dissolution of the senses an elements can take either a few days or as long as a week or two. He recommends that friends and family read to a dying person through the last few days and weeks. Reading, even when the person is asleep, reminds dying people of who they are. What is read should be thoughtfully chosen. The newspaper is probably not the best idea. Poems or letters may serve, or religious texts if scripture is meaningful to the dying person.

At the beginning of this chapter we mention that Americans have few customs or rituals that can guide us through these last days of life. Rinpoche suggests an intriguing practice: he recommends that people prepare a *Dharma box*. This box should contain instructions about medications and end-of-life preferences but should also contain mementos, poems, prayers, letters, and objects that are meaningful for the person preparing to die. Friends and family can select these objects, letters, poems, and so on, read them aloud and talk about them, constantly reminding the dying person of what life has meant. Rinpoche calls the people who choose to be with the dying on this journey *Dharma friends*.

Not everyone can be or needs to be a Dharma friend. Some people who offer help come with their own need to say goodbye or to forgive or be forgiven. People who stay through the entire experience can choose to participate in this bedside ritual. Aside from reading, there's not much to be done. A Dharma friend is one who can remain centered and present and not spend time trying to fix the situation.

Bedside Manners

Those who choose to join a dying person on their final journey often have no idea how to do it. Families need time for their regular duties, time to grieve, time for self-care, and time for being with the patient. The Metta-Institute was established to train professionals as End of Life Practitioners. Its founder, Frank Ostaseski, has outlined five precepts for companions of the dying at: https://fiveinvitations.com/.

The first precept is to welcome everything and push away nothing. It takes courage and flexibility to sit with dying people. The job is to listen, to trust the experience, and to stay open to whatever unfolds. Part of the task is to pay careful attention to what's happening, to words and nonverbal cues, to changes in energy and pain, and to all the cues and signals that emerge, without trying to change or solve things.

The second precept is to bring to the experience our whole selves, our fears, and our love. We need to attend to what's going on inside ourselves as we discover how to be with someone who's experiencing pain, fear, or grief. Too often we adopt a strategy of mutual pretense to get through the process of someone's death. Trying to be warm and upbeat can be far more wearing than allowing our own pain and fear to surface when they bubble up. Stuffing your own feelings down again and again can build a barrier, blocking your own strength and compassion. You may, in this journey, need to find someone to support you, too.

Here's the third precept: don't wait. When you're waiting for someone to die, you're often full of anxiety and worry about what's going to happen next. Waiting for death can mean missing out on the present. If you need to say, "I love you," do it. If you need forgiveness, ask for it. Take the opportunities that arise along the way to strengthen your relationship.

The fourth precept is to find a place of peace in the middle of things. At Hospice of Santa Barbara, for instance, volunteers are taught to take a moment before entering a dying person's room. Find your center, your balance, your sense of calm. Breathe, pray, meditate.

Finally, cultivate an open mind unbounded by roles, regulations, and expectations. No one knows what's going to happen, but we can "not know" together, staying close to the situation, and letting our actions be guided by immediate experience rather than by our expectations or judgments.

In the spirit of not waiting, it's important to find expression for a few crucial sentiments. Both dying people and those who surround them often feel the need to ask for forgiveness, to express their love and appreciation, to say goodbye, and to know that it's okay to die. Monica Williams-Murphy and Kristin Murphy make a strong argument for friends and family to facilitate the reunion of a dying person with someone with whom they feel the need to reconcile, if that's possible. Unaddressed feelings can cause a person to hang on, hoping for closure, and they likewise can become regrets for survivors ("He never really got to say goodbye"). They also argue that letting someone know it's okay to die is an essential assertion of living and dying peacefully.

Anticipatory Grieving

At the same time that family and friends mount an effort to care for and accompany a dying person, they begin to grieve for their loss. It's a natural reaction to the expectation of death and includes mourning, planning, and beginning to reorganize one's own psychosocial life. The recognition that a loved one is dying activates mourning not only for that loss, but also for past and future losses. Each step along the way can arouse fresh grief. A husband loses the help he used to have with daily life, social activities, financial matters, and relationships. Later, he realizes that he grieves that fact that his wife can no longer be his counsel, or express her love in the many ways he misses (no morning hug or evening shoulder massage). Finally, he'll lose both the comfort of her presence and the predictability of the routines and patterns that organized his life, even as she was dying. Caring for a dying person can consume every free moment and, once the person has died, there's no way to easily reorganize one's time and activities.

There is some debate about whether these anticipatory reactions can lessen the burden of postmortem grief; but it's clear that, given a long trajectory in the terminal phase, anticipatory grieving can wear on the relationship for both patient and caregiver. Help, respite, and self-care—including good nutrition, exercise, social support, and a chance for relaxation—are vital to dealing well with an extended trajectory of a loved one's death. Skills such as delegation, communication, and collaboration can be indispensable to the health and well-being of survivors.

The symptoms of postmortem grief, such as sadness, anger, forgetfulness, depression, and dread of death itself, also present as the symptoms of anticipatory grief. Combined with the exhaustion that comes from caring for someone who's dying, the entire situation can become overwhelming. Watching someone you love suffer is hard enough. Often, survivors feel relief when someone dies, only to experience guilt upon noticing their relief.

All of these feelings and reactions are both normal and common. Although researchers have been studying anticipatory grief for nearly 75 years, the findings we have are still full of conflict. No one can say for certain that anticipatory grief makes later bereavement easier or harder. We have no conclusive data about whether longer periods of illness (over six months) make it any easier or harder to adjust after the person dies. Personal factors—such as personality traits, attitudes toward death, beliefs about an afterlife, and the health and well-being of survivors—may all be at play in bereavement.

Anticipatory grief doesn't mean you've given up, and it doesn't make caregiving any easier. It's important to take care of yourself and seek support and counseling when you need it. The Visiting Nurse Service of New York recommends that caregivers use their grief to help settle unresolved issues and to plan for the end of their own lives. They encourage caregivers to seek group or individual counseling, in person, online, or on the phone. They warn against putting your own life on hold and encourage meeting with friends and doing things you enjoy as often as possible as you go along. Dying doesn't mean your life has to be unrelentingly grim. There can still be moments of joy and happiness even in little things such as a walk or wheelchair ride in the fresh air, a good laugh over a TV show, or a good cry over a movie. Grand gestures aren't required and may not be helpful. Just bringing your whole self, with your sadness, fear, joy, and pain, is all you need in order to be a good companion to a dying person. You can visit the Visiting Nurse Service of New York's website at www.vnsny.org/article/5-steps-for-dealing-with-anticipatory-grief.

References for This Chapter:

Kerr, C. W., Donnelly, J. P., Wright, S. T., Kaszczak, S., Banas, A., Grant, P. C., & Luczkiewicz, D. C. (2014). End of life dreams and visions: A longitudinal study of hospice patients' experiences. *Journal of Palliative Care, 17*(3), 1-8.

Reynolds, L., & Botha, D. (2006). Anticipatory grief: Its nature, impact, and reasons for contradictory findings. *Counseling Psychology and Health, 2*(2), 15-26.

Rinpoche, A. (2010). *Dying with confidence: A Tibetan Buddhist guide to preparing for death.* E. Cahoon, (Ed.), A. Graboski (Trans). Boston, MA: Wisdom Books.

CHAPTER 12

CULTURAL LESSONS:
DIVERSE IDEAS ABOUT LIFE, LOVE, AND DEATH

1 previous chapters we have presented data about racial and ethnic pref-
rences regarding the end of life, the use of healthcare facilities, and the
mportance of the family in decision making. In this chapter, we explore
ifferences in beliefs, rituals, and customs regarding death among several
f the largest American minority groups. We also look at the differences in
ttitudes toward death and dying that are associated with some of the major
eligions in the United States.

frican American Culture

The end-of-life practices of African Americans have been shaped
oth by their African heritage and by the history of slavery and discrimina-
on many have experienced in the United States, in parts of South America,
d throughout much of the Caribbean. In most African traditions, death
seen as a natural part of the lifecycle. Death is framed as the moment of
ansit from the world of the living to the spirit world. Extended funeral
tuals can last for days, with careful treatment of the body. There is great
verence for the dead; rituals are often mandated on anniversaries or upon
change of seasons.

Funeral traditions are accorded great significance in most African
aditions, and care is always provided by the community. These beliefs
d customs have their modern equivalents. In African American church-
, funeral services are frequently called *homegoings* and death is referred

to as a *passing*. Elaborate funerals, accompanied by music and often vivid expressions of grief and mourning, are common, as is the display of the deceased's body.

Compared to other groups, African Americans are more likely to rely on the family and less likely to look to hospice and other end-of-life services. As noted before, African Americans are less likely to have advance directives and DNRs. They are more likely to depend upon family and close friends to tend to the dying and more often express ideas such as "it's up to God now." These facts are often explained by the arguments that, in comparison to many other groups, African Americans more frequently turn to God for support when dealing with health issues and that African Americans have experienced more struggle and suffering than other people, resulting in an increased acceptance of and ability to cope with death and dying. It's also true that the healthcare system in the U.S. provides less than optimal care to low-income patients, a factor which is more applicable to African Americans due to income inequality. Such families may not have health insurance or a consistent family practitioner. African Americans have experienced discrimination in many institutions and have little reason to trust the healthcare system or believe that healthcare professionals will see their lives as valuable and important.

African American funerals are usually quite expressive and tend to reflect a legacy of struggle. Music is an important dimension of African American funerals, sometimes expressing a joy at being released from earthly suffering. Perhaps the most well-known expression of this sentiment is the New Orleans funeral procession in which death is belittled and scorned. Death is treated as a passing moment. Life is celebrated instead with music, dancing, singing, and often a cold beer or two in the local bar at the end of the parade. Celebrations such as this allow people to get past the sadness and anger, helping to ease the grief.

Hispanic Culture

It's hard to overestimate the role of family among Hispanic people, though customs may vary by nationality. Family is the foundation of Hisanic life and, not surprisingly, families usually care for the dying at home. Most American Hispanics are of Mexican or Puerto Rican heritage, although large communities of Cubans, South Americans, and Central Americans are scattered across the American landscape. Perhaps the most prominent Mexican tradition is *la Dia de los Muertos* (the Day of the Dead), which expresses, with irony and sarcasm, a basic attitude about the connectedness of life and death, reminding us that death comes to us all, rich and poor.

The memorial aspect of *la Dia de los Muertos* reflects the importance of honoring the dead. Families meet in cemeteries to clean and decorate the graves of loved ones, in celebration of the return of the dead. Tradition dictates that the dead come home for a meal of bread and sweets, reinforcing the idea that death only represents a transition and that the dead are still in relationship with the living. The prevailing mood is of a festival where grief is not welcomed. It's believed that sorrow places a burden on the journey of the dead from the spirit world.

People of Hispanic origin are now the largest ethnic minority in the United States. In California and Texas, they now constitute 48% of the population. Many funeral homes, therefore, offer special services for Hispanic clients. Mexican American funerals, most of which are Catholic, encourage strong emotional responses. Funerals begin with a wake followed by a traditional Mass. There are then nine days of mourning, during which the family lights candles at the altar. At the wake and after the Mass, family and friends eat and drink together. Children are included in all these rituals and are taught about death and the afterlife from an early age. Graveside services are also an important part of the funeral. Traditional in-ground burial is preferred by most Hispanic families, who will return to the grave to remember the dead.

Hispanic families may want to be involved in the dressing and washing of the body. Often, they ask for the body to be displayed overnight and decorate the casket with photos, jewelry, and religious pictures. Flowers are not a major part of the funeral display and, because the cost of a funeral is often a burden, it is not uncommon for mourners to tuck money in sympathy cards for the family. Wakes at home may last overnight. People drink and eat throughout the night while they pray and weep. At the funeral, heartbreaking melodies encourage tears. Sometimes, a large decal is placed on the back of someone's car and dedicated to the deceased, or a shrine may be built in the place where the person was killed (for example, near an automobile accident). At the party after the funeral, bottle rockets are launched to scare away bad spirits. The party becomes a celebration of life.

Asian American Culture

Asian Americans comprise a highly diverse group, with individuals tracing their heritage to China, Japan, Korea, and the many countries of South Asia and Southeast Asia. Traditional religions such as Hinduism, Buddhism, and Shinto are practiced alongside Christianity and Islam. Respect for one's ancestors is a cornerstone of Asian cultures; the living continue to speak to the deceased through prayer and ritual. Coexisting with a love and respect for the dead is a fear of ill-willed spirits. Both Japanese and Chinese cultures honor their ancestors and, at the same time, attempt to create distance between the spirits of the dead and their descendants. Many of these cultures may focus more attention on the treatment of the dead than on support for bereaved survivors.

Chinese and Japanese cultures encourage survivors to maintain ties with the dead, to talk to them, and to pray to them. Families often retain the ashes of the dead in the home or at the family gravesite where they can be visited frequently. Paper offerings symbolize money, housing, food, and even cars or telephones that the ancestors can use in the afterlife. These offerings are usually burned during the funeral and on memorial days such as the Lunar New Year or the Japanese Festival of the Lanterns.

Traditional Chinese funerals are planned using the Chinese almanac to guide the choice of an appropriate date. Invitations are issued for the funeral, and RSVPs are expected. If guests can't attend, flowers and a white envelope containing money may be sent to the home or the funeral. Funerals are a solemn occasion, calling for dark clothes, unless the deceased is over 80. Mourners may wear white at the funeral of an elder, as a sign of the celebration of a long life.

Chinese funerals begin with a wake, which may be held at the home, at a temple, or at a mortuary. A wake may last for several days. Family and friends purchase elaborate floral wreaths for the wake and bring white, cash-filled envelopes to be placed in the robe worn by the deceased. Pictures, flowers, and candles are placed on and around the body. The family often distributes red envelopes with a coin inside to ensure that guests travel home safely, along with a piece of candy and a handkerchief. None of these items are actually taken home but are used at the funeral or along the way home. The funeral procession takes place after the ceremony and may be accompanied by loud music to keep unwanted spirits at bay.

Mourners wear somber clothing and cloth armbands for the entire mourning period, which can last up to 100 days, depending on the status of the deceased. The period of mourning is longest for immediate family members. Prayers are said once a week and ceremonies are held. The number of ceremonies depends on the family's financial resources. Regardless of the family's financial situation, though, the funeral of an elder must be carried out in accordance with the person's social status, even if the family has to go into debt. Doing things properly is believed to ward off any ill effects that the death might otherwise have on the survivors.

For traditional Chinese mourners, everything is prescribed: the placement of objects; the position of survivors for the wake; and the order of survivors in the funeral procession. Red cloth is used to cover the statues of Chinese gods in the home; white is used over the doorway; yellow covers the face of the deceased. No one is allowed to *wear* red though, as this is the color of happiness. A practitioner of Feng Shui is often consulted in choosing the site for the burial. A great variety of food and drink is required at both the wake and the funeral, including pork, duck, chicken, rice, fruit, tea, and wine, as well as *jai*, a dish that contains a variety of mushrooms, fungi, moss, seeds, bean threads, and other vegetables. Most disconcerting to the outsider, children who die must be mourned in silence, and prayers are never offered for a child. This practice reflects the tradition that older people should not ever show respect for younger ones.

Like Chinese funerals, Japanese customs include wakes, funerals, burial ceremonies, and periods of mourning. Nearly all Japanese who die are cremated. At the wake, people wear somber clothes and bring black and silver envelopes full of cash. Most wakes and funerals are performed according to Buddhist tradition, though some are Shinto. More about the Buddhist customs and beliefs will be detailed later in this chapter. At a Japanese funeral, guests again wear somber clothes and bring a monetary gift in a traditional envelope, avoiding an amount that contains the number four (which means death in Japanese). The envelope is placed in a tray and never handed directly to the family. Only family members attend the cremation and burial ceremonies. After the funeral, family and friends generally hold a memorial service every seventh day for 49 days and then on the anniversary of the first, second, and sixth years after the death.

Native American Culture

Among Native Americans, customs vary widely according to tribal traditions. One belief held in common is that the spirits of the dead, though they've passed into the spirit world, continue to affect the living. Historically, customs have included sophisticated embalming and mummification and either leaving the deceased in a cave, sending the body down a river in a canoe, or burying it in tombs lavishly furnished with items the deceased will need in the spirit world. Most tribes practice the burial of food, weapons, jewelry, and other objects of everyday life. Certain rituals are common across tribes, such as gathering in a circle, communal smoking of a pipe, and certain customs designed to keep ghosts away from the living. The entire tribe attends the wake and the funeral, where providing food and drink for everyone is an important requirement. Funerals can be quite large, as the entire local tribal community is expected to attend.

The family generally washes and dresses the body and places it in a shroud or a wooden casket. The body may be honored for several days before the funeral. The body is never left alone before being buried. A medicine man may perform a ceremony. Tribes usually have customs dictating not only what is to be worn, eaten, and sung, but also how long the survivors will stay in mourning. Christian customs, ceremonies, and practices are of ten intermingled with Native rituals.

Reverence for the dead, coupled with a respect born of fear, is prevalent among Native American people, and many disputes have arisen over burial grounds being disturbed by outsiders for real estate development. Tribes with permanent settlements, such as the Navajo and Hopi, traditionally experience more fear of the dead than do nomadic tribes. Historically, nomadic people have left their dead behind as they moved from place to place. Some tribes, such as the Navajo and Apache, avoid the dead, burying them quickly, and spending little time in mourning, due perhaps, to worry that restless spirits resent the living or to a desire not to disturb the spirit's journey as it makes its way to the next world.

These are just a few of the many variations in attitudes, rituals, and customs practiced in the United States today. Among the individuals of each ethnic group you'll also find major differences in religious beliefs and practices. There are Chinese American Protestants, Mexican American Muslims, and Native American Catholics. Many of the differences between people of the same nationality, ethnicity, or race have to do with the religious beliefs that they don't hold in common.

Christian Practice

Many of the groups we've discussed practice a mix of Christianity and traditional customs, including African Americans, Hispanic Americans, Native Americans, and many Asian subgroups. Christians profess a belief in the resurrection of the body and an everlasting life. At the end of time, many Christians believe, Jesus will return to raise the body and to judge both the living and the dead. Some Christians believe that they'll need a physical body from this life when Judgment Day arrives and they're assigned to either heaven or hell. In some modern forms of Christianity, the resurrection of the physical body and the idea of hell have lost their central place in the belief structure. Many denominations now focus on the gospel, the good news of an abundant, eternal life and a loving God.

Christianity: Catholicism

Among Catholics, a third option exists at Judgment Day: purgatory. Purgatory is a temporary state where, according to Jean-Pierre Isbouts (2014),

> . . .very few people are allowed into heaven upon death without doing penance. Purgatory is, therefore, a sort of halfway house, a probationary state between death and heaven, with facilities that were believed to be not very comfortable. The idea of purgatory was a fairly novel invention, developed at the Council of Lyon in 1245. Some clerics argued at the time that it could take many thousands of years before one was admitted to heavenly bliss.

A traditional Catholic receives last rites as death draws near. A priest is summoned to the bedside of the dying person to hear a last confession, administer Holy Communion, and absolve the dying person of sin. Because Catholics and some Protestants profess the resurrection of the body, some Catholics feel uncomfortable with organ donation. Others, though, now frame it as a final charitable act. Catholics believe in the efficacy of good works to help believers get into heaven.

Here's what you're likely to experience if you attend a Catholic funeral. It begins with a vigil, or wake, which is a prayer service, often presided over by a priest, beginning the night before the funeral. Because the formal funeral service is reserved for a celebration of Mass conducted by a priest, eulogies and tributes are taken care of at the vigil, often accompanied by a sermon that incorporates events and remembrances from the lifetime of the deceased. The body is usually present at both the vigil and the service. If the body is then cremated (which is not forbidden today), the ashes are preserved. Catholics don't scatter the ashes of the dead, believing that keeping the ashes together may allow one's body to be present at the resurrection. Food and drink are usually offered to mourners after both the wake and the funeral service. You'll be expected to wear dark, conservative clothing a the funeral and to send flowers for the service or make memorial donations to charity.

Christianity: Protestantism

While each of the Protestant denominations has distinct doctrines and practices, most Protestant funerals revolve around the entry of the deceased into the afterlife, along with testimonials and remembrances about the person's life. Often, if the body is intact, the family may arrange for viewing. Friends and family come and go to pay their last respects for short periods of time. Most Protestants don't pray for the souls of the dead, because nothing more can be done to save them. The fate of the deceased on Judgment Day will depend on the choices they made in life.

Funerals are held at home or in a church and usually include eulogies, instrumental music, the singing of hymns, and readings from the Bible. In some services, mourners are welcome to offer spontaneous memories of the deceased. Flowers, sympathy cards, and charitable donations are typically sent by the mourners. After the funeral, there may be a graveside service. Cremations are generally conducted before the funeral and the ashes are present at the service. There is wide variation in how ashes are handled, as we will detail in the chapter on funerals.

After the service, family and friends usually gather at the home of the deceased, where the family provides food and drink. Mourners may linger for quite a while, exchanging stories and remembrances. Both laugher and weeping are common at these events. People often enjoy the party as a celebration of the life of the deceased and connect with members of the extended family who've traveled to the funeral.

Judaism

Beliefs about the existence of an afterlife vary widely among Jews. These include the belief that the soul inherits no afterlife but, rather, returns to its source, a kind of oblivion called *Sheol*, a shadow world where the soul slowly fades away. Others believe in the possibility of the soul's resurrection in the final judgment. Jewish customs don't emphasize the fate of any one person, focusing instead on God's preservation of the Israelites as a people. Most religious Jews do believe that, after the death of the body, the soul goes to be with God.

Jewish tradition teaches that the spirit hovers around the body until after the body is buried. A Jewish funeral is more concerned with honoring the deceased than with the feelings of the mourners. Sensitive care of the body and the dignity of the deceased are paramount. From the time a person dies, someone stays with the body to comfort the soul by reading passages from the Book of Psalms. The body is washed and dressed, but embalming and the use of cosmetics is contrary to Jewish law. Jews are buried in a simple white linen shroud and are dressed in a hat, shirt, pants, shoes, coat—all made of white linen—and, for men, a prayer shawl. Metal caskets aren't permitted. The casket has holes drilled in the bottom to ensure that the body returns to the earth as soon as possible. Cremation is forbidden, as is the viewing of the body, both customs being seen as undignified. The only acceptable burial is in the ground, and this must be completed within 24 hours, according to rabbinical law. Autopsy is also forbidden in the Jewish tradition, though one might get a dispensation for certain kinds of special circumstances.

For example, Dale and Fabian had spent a beautiful morning with their son and his wife snorkeling off a small boat Panama. As he was getting back into the boat, Fabian had a heart attack. At first, Dale thought it was a seizure, but as events unfolded they started CPR. They kept it up for 25 minutes before they let him go. Fabian never regained consciousness. Dale remembers leaning over him and saying goodbye, telling him how much she loved him. They returned to a remote village on the boat with his body. It was an odd experience, but having that much time to just be with him and each other was healing:

> When we arrived, our "nightmare" began. The police were called. They interviewed us, but no arrangements were made for the body. After hours, they were able to locate a medical examiner who transferred the body to a truck, but didn't say where they were going: just to a large city three

hours away. They wouldn't let Dale ride in the truck, so she called a taxi. While we waited, they tried to leave with the body. My son and I had to block the vehicle and neither the police nor the villagers tried to stop us. Five hours later, we followed the body to the city.

It took three days to deal with civic and state authorities. An autopsy was required, even though it was against our religious beliefs, and Dale had to identify the body again, a painful experience. Once the embassy took over, things went more smoothly. Dale [said] "It is hard to lose a husband so early, but Fabian lived life to the fullest, and I'm doing what I can to continue that legacy."

Jewish funerals may take place at a funeral home, a temple, or a cemetery. At an Orthodox funeral, mourners traditionally make a tear in their clothing or, if the service is non-Orthodox, in a black ribbon pinned to the lapel. Eulogies are offered at the beginning of the service as well as at the gravesite, where it is customary for mourners to throw three shovels-full of dirt into the grave.

Mourning officially ends on the seventh day after the funeral. During these seven days, Orthodox Jews refrain from bathing, wearing jewelry, or shaving, and people sit on low stools or on the floor to show that they're "brought low" by grief. No mourning or burial is ever held on the Sabbath, however. During the seven days after the service, the family "sits shiva" and receives visitors. In the Orthodox tradition, no greetings are exchanged, but family members may lead a prayer service. Visitors are expected to cook and clean for the family during Shiva. Mourning is observed for a year in an Orthodox family. Even in less Orthodox families, the children of the deceased continue to say Kaddish—a traditional Jewish prayer of praise for God—for an entire year during prayer services. Jews are required to commemorate the death of a close relative on the four days of remembrance that occur during the course of the year and on the person's birthday. At one year after the death, the headstone is unveiled, prayers are offered, and there may be a brief eulogy.

Islam

Followers of Islam believe in the immortality of the soul and the in evitability of a judgment day, where one will be either welcomed into one o the seven levels of paradise or condemned to one of the seven levels of hel Muslims also believe, however, that God is compassionate and just and tha the archangel Gabriel may intercede for those who have been condemned saving them from eternal punishment.

Islamic religious law, which forbids cremation, calls for the buria of the dead as soon as possible. The eyes and mouth are closed, and th body is washed three times with warm water and then placed in a shrou The shroud is tied with ropes at the top of the head and on the upper bod of the deceased, the lower body, and the feet. The deceased is often burie within 24 hours, with the body laid on its right side in the grave, facin toward Mecca.

Same-sexed adults in the immediate family may take the task c washing and wrapping the body. Mourners are allowed to visit the body be fore the service. There is rarely an open casket at a Muslim funeral. Praye are said for the forgiveness of the deceased and for all Islam. Clothes ar somber, and headscarves are required for women. Flowers aren't sent to th funeral but are accepted by the family during the 40-day mourning perio Autopsies are forbidden, but organ donations are often looked upon as final act of charity.

At the funeral, mourners form three lines for prayer. Men stand i the front line, women in the back, and children in between. Prayers are reci ed in the prayer room, not in the mosque proper, and only men are allowe in the procession to the graveyard and at the burial site. A layer of wood c stones is placed over the body to protect it from direct contact with the eart and then each of the mourners places three handfuls of dirt in the grave. Le traditional mosques have relaxed the rules about women at the gravesite, b conservative mosques still observe them.

After the burial, the family receives visitors, and the communit provides food for the first three days. Weeping is common, but dramati estures of grief are not condoned, as they reflect a lack of faith that Allah as chosen an appropriate moment for death. Only a small, modest head-one is placed on the grave, as lavishness is considered a sin that can lead damnation. Candles, flowers, or other offerings are not used at either the aneral or the grave.

uddhism

Like Christianity, Buddhism has many interpretations and sects, but the major tenets that unite them are called the "Four Noble Truths." These include the belief that all human life is full of pain and suffering in an ardu-us cycle of death and rebirth. Only enlightenment can end the cycle. The second truth is that desire for personal satisfaction is the cause of all one's uffering, and the third truth is that detachment from desire will bring deliv-ance. The fourth truth lays out the eightfold path to enlightenment through ght understanding, right resolve, right speech, right conduct, right effort, ght livelihood, right mindfulness, and right meditation. By making peace ith our emotions through surrender, Buddhists believe we can find joy in orrow. There is no heaven in Buddhism, only the attainment of Nirvana, a ate of consciousness that is accompanied by happiness, peace, and fulfill-ent. Buddhists don't believe in the survival of the individual personality or lf beyond the grave. You can find out more about the beliefs of American uddhists at: https://rk-world.org/dharmaworld/dw_2011julyseptdramatic-owth.aspx

Death is seen by Buddhists as a way to awaken to the truth. Medi-tion on one's own death can bring enlightenment. A good death is one that filled with peace and calm rather than fear and struggle. During the days st after death, Buddhists believe there is still an opportunity for enlight-ment. Family and friends will pray for the enlightenment of the deceased that person is passing through the *bardos* of the afterlife. A bardo is a ace between realities, such as the one between one life and another where le must face one's karmic demons before being incarnated again. All sects rform similar funeral rites, partly built around supporting the deceased in e transition from this life to the next.

As people near death, friends and family gather to encourage them to be calm, to meditate, and to find peace and acceptance. For this reason devout Buddhists don't choose any pain medication that would put them in an unconscious state. The body of the deceased is left undisturbed until it is cold (a minimum of four hours), as the soul is thought not to leave the body immediately. Some groups wait as long as four days before burial. Once cold, the body is washed and dressed in ordinary, everyday clothes. Organ donation, embalming, and cremation are all acceptable. Ashes may be kept in an urn or scattered.

Memorial services may be arranged on the third, seventh, forty-ninth, or hundredth day after the death. A wake is held with an open casket. Photos, flowers, candles, fruit, and incense are placed near the casket. Chants about the fleeting nature of life often take place at the wake. On the morning of the funeral, monks perform the last rites and chant contemplative verses. At the funeral, mourners wear white. The ceremony is simple and solemn. The casket or cremated remains are placed at the front of the room surrounded by flowers, candles, fruit, incense, and photos of the Buddha and the deceased. Mourners approach the altar, bow their heads, and press their hands together before taking a seat. Everyone may chant and pray, and there may be eulogies and a sermon.

Mourners are encouraged to send gifts to charity. Sometimes mourners walk with a stick to symbolize their grief. Bells or gongs may be rung. Food gifts are considered inappropriate. A mourning period of 90 days is traditional, but there are few rules or customs that the bereaved must follow.

Hinduism

Like Buddhists, Hindus believe in reincarnation and successive rounds of birth and death. The soul, which is considered divine, continues to repeat the cycle of life and death, seeking to discover the divine within the self, until it detaches from the very idea of self and, ultimately, becomes one with the divine. Death is not regarded as an occasion for grief and sorrow, which can impede the departed soul's journey toward its next incarnation, but rather as progress toward *mukti*, the final freedom from this otherwise continuous cycle of death and rebirth. Meditation on the ever-changing nature of existence, a practice that can lead to enlightenment, is appropriate at burials or cremations in response to the presence of the dead body.

Hindus prefer to die at home, surrounded by friends and family. When a person dies, the body is placed on a grass mat, if possible, then washed in a mixture of yogurt, milk, and clarified butter, and finally wrapped in a shroud with the big toes tied together and the hands placed in a position of prayer. The family often builds a shelter for a fire as part of the ceremony. The service is referred to as a wake and there is usually an open casket. Guests are expected to view the body but are not allowed to touch it. Guests send flowers; however, gifts of food are forbidden. The remains are kept at home until they are cremated, being placed in the crematorium fire feet first. The body of a child or a saint is buried; children and saints can immediately move forward without the body being destroyed, having been less attached to it during life. One of the authors recently attended the cremation of the King of Ubud, an old regency within the country of Indonesia.

The royal family, despite Ubud's occupation by European and Japanese powers through much of the nineteenth and twentieth centuries, remains a cornerstone of Ubud society. Luckily, Larry and Judy were able to view the procession from the balcony of a local gemologist's shop. There was a parade of clans and temple members, as well as members of the royal family, [a procession] through the main street, each group dressed in outfits ranging from traditional robes and funeral clothes to tee shirts with the names of their temples on the back. There were thousands of mourners, either lining the main street or taking part in the procession.

After the temple and clan groups came the princesses, granddaughters of the king, carried aloft on structures that looked like Mardi Gras floats, adorned with crepe paper and papier-mâché flowers. The floats that passed by were each borne on the shoulders of several young men. Next, the bands of drummers marched by, followed by a two-story float in the shape of a black bull with golden horns. We were told that the body of the king was going to be cremated inside the bull. The bull was built on a bamboo lattice carried by maybe 60 young men who lifted the float up, ran like the dickens for about a block, set the float down, and were immediately replaced by a new set of bearers.

The finale began with the arrival of a five-story float in the shape of a tower. On the top of the fourth story, a balcony held a priest, the casket of the deceased king, and the new king. The young king smiled and waved at the enthusiastic crowd, then sat down on the casket, swung his legs over the balcony, leaned back, and started taking selfies! Watching the parade, we imagined that the deceased king was being given such a send-off that surely his next incarnation would be another good and long life.

The funeral parade, Ubud

After the funeral, family members wash, change clothes, and gather for dinner. In India, ashes are submerged in the Ganges the next day. American Hindus often ship the ashes to India for this purpose, although there are rivers in other countries that are now considered acceptable. The family stays at home, and receives visitors for 13 days after the funeral. Children participate in all of the rites and customs, as they are taught to understand death from an early age

Conclusion

This amazing variety of beliefs, customs, and rituals reflects the persistence of the many diverse assumptions about living and dying that have become a hallmark of American life. Many funeral homes and mortuaries are now sensitive to, and happy to serve the needs of families from different countries of origin, unique traditions, and contrasting religions. Families from some of the older, more traditional cultures may be leading the way both to home care for the dying in America and to the involvement of families in caring for the body after death.

We realize that these descriptions may not apply to particular sects within a religion. Our main goal has been to highlight some of the differences among the major religions as they are traditionally practiced. In a later chapter on grief and bereavement, we'll discuss how important it can be for healthcare professionals and counselors to understand a family's distinct interpretation of religious and cultural traditions.

References for This Chapter:

Byock, Ira (2014). *The four things that matter most: A book about living* (10th ed.). New York, NY: Atria Books–Simon and Schuster.

Isbouts, J.-P. (2016). *Ten prayers that changed the world: Extraordinary stories of faith that shaped the course of history.* Washington, DC: National Geographic.

Moreman, C. M. (2010). *Beyond the threshold: Afterlife beliefs and experiences in world religions.* New York, NY: Rowman & Littlefield publishers, Inc.

PART FOUR

What happens after we die?

CHAPTER 13

CARING FOR THE BODY:
FUNERALS, MEMORIALS, AND CELEBRATIONS

The funeral-service industry has grown exponentially worldwide, yet the general public knows little about its inner workings. Many of us think of funeral home as the first call when a family member dies. Using funeral homes to take care of so many details at a time of intense grief and sorrow makes sense. There are many functions that a funeral home performs, from picking up the body, preparing the body for burial, to helping plan a ceremony and the burial, and more.

How does the funeral industry operate? And what are some of the alternatives? Very few of us wholly understand what it means to interact with a funeral industry that is now dominated by global enterprises and in the business to make a profit. Many of the funeral homes and cemeteries that were once privately owned by families or nonprofit organizations have been taken over by profit-minded, global corporations. The more services and goods they sell to grieving families, the higher their profits. In fact, most funeral directors receive remuneration based entirely on sales commissions. This newer, more aggressive system means higher prices for funeral services, burials, and cremations. Understanding the funeral industry, traditional funerals, and alternative ways to bury loved ones allows us to explore all of our options as we make our plans.

In 2013, a documentary by PBS on the economics of the funeral industry estimated that the U.S. funeral market has become a $20.7-billion per-year industry. An illustration of what this means is the National Funeral Directors Association's January, 2018 announcement of their upcoming event in sunny Florida, promoting it as "The Profession's Hottest Cremation Conference." Participants in the gathering were promised that they would learn how to communicate the "value of the funeral; boosting the profitability of your cremation business." It's no surprise that a 2013 report by Bloomberg showed the large Houston-based Service Corporation International (SCI) overcharging its customers for traditional services by 42% more than independent funeral homes, while at the same time putting these family-owned funeral homes out of business. This, of course, doesn't imply that all of the people working for these for-profit firms are hard-hearted.

Women in the Funeral Industry

Like many other profit-centered institutions, the funeral industry isn't completely defined by its tough business side, because it does have sympathetic heart for the loss and grief that people experience. According to CBS news, consumers need to be aware, however, that a show of compassion can still bear a cost. We discuss the costs of funerals and burials in the next section.

One change in the funeral industry may reinforce its caring side. Women are entering the business and redefining the industry. Leah Millin, senior funeral director in the United States, views her job as a privilege, while Jillian Rutherford, a funeral director in England, helps families celebrate the lives of loved ones and still sheds tears behind the scenes. More women now hold senior management positions, overseeing many funeral homes. In 2015, *Fortune* magazine published an article by Anne Fisher outlining how women in the business were teaching others how to be more compassionate and nurturing. For more information about these developments, read Anne Fisher's article in *Fortune*: "Why your funeral will probably be run by woman" (http://fortune.com/2015/08/20/funeral-directors-women).

Publicly traded corporations such as SCI—the largest funeral corporation in the country, with $550.3 million in annual operating income—offer more job opportunities to women than do small, independent funeral homes. For the past century or so, women were not considered good can didates for funeral directors, given that some of the tasks, such as lifting and transporting bodies, require upper-body strength. In the 1990s, only a small number of women graduated from the Worsham College of Mortuary Science. Today more than half of the students there are women. In fact, the National Funeral Directors Association reports that more than 60% of mortuary-science students in the United States are women.

The 2015 *Fortune* article, "Why your funeral will probably be run by a woman," emphasized the interest of women in mortuary work as a second career. Funeral directors spend only 10% of their time with the decedent, performing tasks such as embalming, while the other 90% is spent with families. Curricula in schools now emphasize courses in sociology and psychology, specifically the psychology of grief. For women, the funeral business is about relationships, social work, counseling, and event planning. Nonetheless, for survivors, a funeral is still an expensive and emotionally difficult task, one that Americans will experience far more frequently in the near future. The United States must cope with 78 million baby boomers as they approach death in the next three decades, and the impact of the baby boomer generation isn't limited to the U.S. It's a worldwide force that already affects the funeral industry abroad, too, especially in Japan.

Baby Boomers and the Funeral Industry

Over the last 15 years, the number of annual deaths in Japan has grown to 1.3 million, a 35% increase in the number of deaths per year. As result, Japan's overburdened crematories are struggling to keep up. Traditional Japanese funerals used to be a communal affair in the neighborhood, with ceremonies performed at home followed by cremation within a day. However, neighborhoods no longer serve as social centers for families, and the price for a traditional funeral is rising. Moreover, with a population that's aging quickly, 30% of families skip the traditional funeral ceremonies altogether. Despite this trend, as the *New York Times* reported in 2017, Japanese crematories have a waiting list, forcing families to wait several days before a body can be cremated.

The new *itai hoteru*, or corpse hotel, as mentioned in Chapter 2, was designed to help families store the body of their loved one until their number comes up. Sleeping on beds or sofas, watching flat-screen TVs, and ordering food, the family typically stays in the room with the body—stored properly in a climate-controlled coffin with a see-through lid—until check-out time. Many of these facilities are full service, with altars, venues to hold small wakes for an extra fee, and a showroom displaying accoutrements for sale. The number of deaths in Japan will peak at 1.7 million in 2040, necessitating a comprehensive change in funeral and burial traditions.

The United States has a similar predicament. Demographic studies have shown that, by 2030, more than 20% of the U.S. population will be 65 or older, compared to less than 13% today. This means that more than 70 million Americans will be over the age of 65. By 2056, the number of people 65 years old and over is expected to become larger than the population under 18. Adding to this crisis, six out of 10 boomers will have more than one chronic illness to manage. The prevalence of chronic disease is increasing in all age groups, but baby boomers will be affected most immediately. We have devoted a whole chapter to the topic of chronic illnesses and certain lifestyle changes that promote wellness and health (Chapter 8).

In Japan, the price for a traditional funeral has risen steeply, now costing about around 1.95 million yen, or $17,690. The cheapest package at one of these corpse hotels in Osaka costs 185,000 yen, or $1,768 (for one night, plus about $100 for each additional night). Prices for traditional funerals in the United States have also climbed, though much cheaper *out of the box* alternatives can now be found.

The Cost of Funerals

In the last two decades, prices for funerals in the United States have gone up dramatically. Many commercials claim that the average price for a traditional funeral is around $6,000. There are many common expenses, however, that aren't included in this figure. The $6,000 figure doesn't include flowers, burial in a cemetery, or a headstone for the grave. The average cost including such additional items may range from $8,000 to $10,000 or even higher. It's important to plan carefully, checking all your options

Although the funeral home may arrange many of the details of the funeral, families need to keep in mind that other, separate businesses must be contacted for additional products or services, from securing a plot and a burial in a cemetery to a headstone, flowers, food, printed handouts for the funeral ceremony, and so on.

Here are the average prices for the goods and services of a funeral home. Typically, a casket costs around $2,300. Embalming and other body preparation will take another $600. The mortuary's service fees will run $1,500, more or less, and in addition it costs about $1,000 for viewing plus the funeral ceremony. There are also miscellaneous charges that might cost up to $600 for a hearse, death certificate, obituary, and so on. At the cemetery, a family can expect to spend at least $2,000 on a grave space and also pay about $1,000 for the work to dig the grave. Every grave needs a grave-marker or a headstone. A grave marker is a flat granite or bronze plaque that is laid into the ground atop of the gravesite. A headstone is typically two feet high and made of two pieces granite rock that sit atop the grave. A grave marker costs about $100, while a headstone costs around $2,000.

Burial vaults and grave liners (also called cement liners) are used to support the soil around the casket to ensure that the ground above the casket won't collapse. It's much more difficult to mow lawns laid over graves without liners. Although these items are not legally mandated, most cemeteries require them. A grave liner usually costs between $700 and $1,000, while a burial vault costs between $900 and $7,000 and can range upward of $13,000. If the funeral director arranges these services and products, the prices can be even higher. Prices also vary quite a bit by location. For example, the price of a traditional funeral in Seattle might range from $4,000 to $6,000, but in Dallas or Chicago it's hard to find funeral home at those prices. Depending on the area, a typical funeral might cost $6,000 to $8,000. Table 12.1 presents the range of prices for a traditional funeral in different cities. These prices include neither the gravesite nor the headstone.

City	Low	High
Seattle	$4,000	$6,000
Los Angeles	$4,300	$8,200
Chicago	$6,300	$9,600
Dallas	$6,000	$10,960
Houston	$6,000	$12,325
New York	$4,300	$12,000
Washington, DC	$5,000	$15,000

For more information see: www.parting.com and www.everplans.com.

Funeral Services and Burials

Mainstream American funerals are characterized as "traditional funeral services" on many websites. A traditional funeral service offers structured formality designed to comfort and support the grieving family. Unless otherwise dictated by religion or custom, the service is scheduled three to six days after the day of the death, to allow time for friends and family to travel and rearrange their activities. The viewing begins one or two nights prior to the service, allowing visitors time to say goodbye and pay their respects. The service itself offers flexibility in terms of religious preference, favorite readings, communal sharing of memories, and the type of flowers and their arrangement. Of course, the type of casket selected by the family can dramatically affect the overall cost.

Although the traditional funeral service is highly structured, families can personalize the service to create meaning and celebrate the unique life of their loved one. On the other hand, high-pressure sales can leave families feeling guilty if they don't choose expensive goods and services. Modern sales and marketing techniques that take advantage of the family's vulnerability at this time can stretch an already tight budget to its limits.

In the coming years, the baby boomers are expected to drive prices even higher. Some predict the cost for an average traditional funeral will climb as high as $12,000. Planning in advance is crucial. Most funeral homes start their sales presentation to the grieving family by pitching their most expensive services and goods, underplaying cheaper options. Because of the internet, we're now able to search for funeral homes that offer reasonably priced funeral services. You can even purchase a casket online. Although the baby boomers will increase the demand for funeral goods and services and, in the process, raise prices in the next couple of decades, we suggest that negotiation can bring prices down considerably, as most mortuary prices include substantial markups. Keep in mind that funeral homes mark up by hundreds or even thousands of dollars. If one place doesn't discount their prices, another place might.

One simple choice for burials is called a *direct or immediate burial,* which doesn't include embalming, formal viewing, or a funeral service. In a package like this, the funeral home picks up the body and transports it to the funeral home, creates the death certificate, obtains a burial permit, then buries the body in a grave at the cemetery. The casket and the cemetery lot are priced separately.

In 2017, the National Funeral Directors Association reported that the number of cremations in 2015 edged out the number of burials in the U.S. for the first time. Cremation is continuing to grow in popularity as it's much less expensive than burial. Prices for cremations, as for burials, can vary considerably between different states and cities and even between different funeral homes in the same town. Some funeral homes charge up to three times more for the same cremation and service. Making a difficult time more complicated, many funeral homes don't show their rates online, forcing grieving families to face sales presentations that pressure them to purchase the more expensive items.

Direct cremations through a funeral home generally cost between $1,000 and $3,000. A cremation through a crematory is a little less expensive, costing between $1,000 and $2,200. Some funeral homes use a third party to cremate the remains, raising the cost to between $2,000 and $4,000.

For this reason, it's important to ask the funeral home director for exact pric es. If cremation is combined with a viewing at the funeral home or a funera service, prices rise accordingly.

The cremated remains may be preserved in a porcelain urn or scat tered in a favorite place, a garden, an ocean, or a river. There are many othe unique ways to feature the remains, including a *reef ball* that helps to restore the ocean's reef habitats for around $3,000 and a compressed gem, in an one of a multitude of colors, cuts, and sizes, for about $20,000. Remain can be sent aloft in an air balloons or even shot into space. The idea is to celebrate the life lived in a way that befits the family.

Green Funerals and Burials

Green is the newest addition to the burgeoning list of funeral op tions. According to the Green Burial Council, a green or natural funera takes into consideration the impact of our burials and cremations on the environment. Green funerals are designed to conserve natural resources, re duce carbon emissions, protect workers' health, and even restore habitat and eco-systems. Green funerals use non-toxic and biodegradable materia for the caskets, shrouds, and urns. The Green Burial Council has lists of pro viders, certification for funeral homes, and more information on product and services that receive the green burial approval.

Of course, green burial is not a new concept; most burials up unt the mid-nineteenth century used natural materials that allow for the decom position and absorption of the body and the coffin into the soil. Jewish an Muslim burials today are still primarily natural, although the burial ground may not be green. A green burial ground is environmentally sustainable allowing the gravesite to return to nature. It offers simplicity, as the body i simply wrapped and buried in a shroud or in a coffin made of natural woo such as pine. It offers a lower cost without the pressure of salesmanshi Lastly, green burials eliminate hazardous chemicals in the embalming pro cess, conserve the hardwood, steel, and copper customarily used in casket and vaults that don't decompose, and preserve the natural landscape. Grave are marked by a native plant, a rock, or a modest plaque.

The Green Burial Council has three different classifications for green burial grounds. The first category is called the *hybrid burial ground*, which can be found in a more conventional cemetery that permits burials without outer burial containers (vaults or grave liners) and allows the use any type of container, including a shroud. The second, greener category is called the *natural burial ground*. This type of burial area prohibits outer containers, embalmed bodies because of the toxic chemicals used, and burial containers made of anything except natural or plant-derived materials. A *conservation burial ground* is the third and greenest option as it most vigorously addresses environmental issues. This type of burial ground offers the benefits of the natural burial, plus it must engage a conservation organization recognized by the IRS as a nonprofit, public charity to ensure long-term stewardship of the land.

In 2018, a simple green burial in Seattle cost between $1,215 and $1,465. The plan includes a direct burial in a biodegradable casket without a graveside service. There are no concrete grave liners or vaults, only native grasses, trees, and shrubs. A graveyard service will raise the price to $1,915. As noted above, many funeral homes that offer green burials don't advertise their prices online, yet they're committed to environmental values. For example, Hillside Memorial Park and Mortuary in Los Angeles, is certified by the Green Burial Council as a conservation burial ground. The director views the park as a green, progressive Jewish cemetery, dedicated to the diversity of the families that patronize it, both Jewish and non-Jewish. Green burials are designed to honor the environment as well as the humanity they serve.

Funeral home prices for green funerals and burials can vary, depending on the area. Check the prices online, if available, and compare them to other funeral homes. The Green Burial Council is a good place to start. You can find it at: http://greenburialcouncil.org.

Cremation

Cremation is the process of burning the body into ash through the use of an open fire. As an alternative to traditional burial, cremation was thought to be reasonably eco-friendly, but a growing concern has emerged about the impact of this practice on the environment. Standard cremation uses natural gas for its burners, releasing greenhouse gases, and vaporizes other chemicals present in the body, releasing them into the air. These chemicals include mercury, dioxins, and furans.

To fully incinerate the body, the furnace must be heated to 1400° to 1800°F and maintained for 60 to 90 minutes. It's important to keep in mind that baby boomers most likely have more mercury amalgams in their bodies from dental fillings, increasing mercury emissions. Some organizations are looking for ways to offset the carbon dioxide released in this process; others point to newer crematories that are more fuel-efficient and release fewer toxins into the environment. Another way to offset carbon emissions is by making a contribution to a carbon fund. When choosing a cremation provider, seek out a facility that monitors their emissions and uses pollutant filters to scrub the emissions they release. For more information, check out www.carbonfund.org.

A recent addition to the options for disposition of the body is *green cremation* (greencremation.com), which relies on water infused with potassium hydroxide to dissolve the soft tissues of the body, leaving only fragments of bone. Although the process may be quieter than an open furnace, it may not be as gentle as some brochures claim. In a procedure developed for the Mayo Clinic, the body is sealed in a pressurized, stainless-steel chamber where the temperature is raised to 350°F, creating intense heat that breaks down (hydrolyzes) the human tissue. Although the process is touted as green and eco-friendly, the Environmental Working Group has designated potassium hydroxide as a moderately hazardous chemical that is a corrosive and hazardous irritant at high levels. Since the bio-cremation process uses a fair amount of this chemical, it's still debatable whether or not this method is a good green alternative for a highly populated planet.

We need to evaluate the different methods for disposition of the body, the various places for burial, the kind of ceremony, what flowers to select, and the materials used to construct a casket and to designate a grave. Flowers are beautiful. They bestow upon us a sense of appreciation and even life at a time of immense grief. Yet even providing flowers for the funeral industry has become a big business. Many environmental and social-justice activists have pointed out the negative effects of growing flowers on a huge, industrial scale. Most flowers are grown as mono-crops in underdeveloped countries, where vast lands and other resources are diverted to supply the funeral industry with flowers. Choosing flowers that are grown wild or in a local facility can be comforting and good for the environment.

There are so many things to consider as we grapple with the various arrangements for a funeral and a burial, such as where and how to bury and whether to arrange a traditional ceremony or personalize the service and the wake. What's everything going to cost? How will we impact the environment? How do we manage life going forward? Within this set of questions and demands, we grieve, plan, search, make decisions, and honor our loved ones.

References for This Chapter:

Al-Othman, H. (2017, Dec. 22). Christmas on the job: Leah Milin, senior funeral director at Co-op funeral care. *Buzz Feed*. Retrieved from https://www.buzzfeed.com/hannahalothman/meet-the-people-you-probably-didnt-realise-will-be-working?utm_term=.jkMKKy2wY#.vuw-ZZm4w0

Fisher, A. (2015, August 5). Why your funeral will probably be run by a woman. *Fortune*, retrieved from http://fortune.com/2015/08/20/funeral-directors-women/

Green Burial Council, retrieved from, http://greenburialcouncil.org/find-a-provider/

Wylie, M. (2017, May 24). Six Feet Under: Why these women chose the saddest profession. Retrieved from *Biz Women*, https://www.bizjournals.com/bizwomen/news/profiles-strategies/2016/05/six-feet-under-why-these-women-chose-the-world-s.html?page=all

CHAPTER 14

GRIEVING: A HEALING APPROACH

Grieving is a universal physiological response to grave loss, but how people express that reaction varies greatly from one culture to another. In some societies, loud weeping and wailing are customary. There are groups in which grieving people don't speak at all and those where the bereaved become enraged or even injure themselves. There may be carefully prescribed roles for men and for women; children are excluded from funerals in some traditions and encouraged to come along in others. Physical distress, however, is part of the grief experience, especially when a death is unexpected or sudden.

Grief often begins with a blow. People say that they felt they'd been punched in the stomach or that their stomach (or heart) fell through the floor. As the initial reaction subsides, people feel agitated or restless: they have trouble eating and sleeping. They can't keep food down and report sensations such as choking or tightness in the chest and throat. Grief comes in waves; it engenders feelings of helplessness and anger and of sadness, loneliness, disorientation, and confusion—a chaotic swarm of reactions.

In the 1970s and 1980s, researchers demonstrated that levels of the powerful hormones known as corticosteroids increase during bereavement and stay elevated for a very long time. Corticosteroids are produced in the adrenal glands, like adrenaline, and released when we sense danger or are under stress. Bereaved people have much higher death rates than the general population. Rates of infection and malignancy during bereavement are 2.5 to five times the national average. Corticosteroids may adversely affect the function of the immune system, leaving survivors more vulnerable to illness.

To survivors, the world may seem suddenly unreal or hideously surreal. They may be confused, anxious, disorganized, and depressed. After a death, sadness and anger, longing and loneliness, guilt and frustration can swirl across the days and weeks. People may find themselves wandering aimlessly, as if searching for something or someone. They might talk incessantly about the deceased or refuse to speak of the person. How people experience and express grief not only varies from one person to another; it can also swing widely over time in the same person. People sometimes even experience great relief and, at other times, a weird sense of euphoria.

Grief reactions may result from many types of loss. You can grieve the loss of a job, an excellent opportunity, or a long-treasured object. People who try to resist or avoid the intense distress caused by grieving may only extend and complicate their grief. Like dying, however, grief doesn't have to be an unremittingly grim experience. Many bereaved people experience positive as well as negative changes after the death of a close family member. Grief is part of an active coping process that can support feelings of autonomy and choice and afford opportunities for resilience and courage. Grieving is a complex phenomenon. It's often paradoxical, with contradictory emotions simultaneously competing for your mind.

Mourning

Mourning follows on the heels of grief. Mourning is a process by which bereaved people learn to live with loss. Survivors need to learn how to reconstruct their lives and build a new normal. *The Handbook of Thanatology* (the study of death) defines mourning as an active process that revolves around four central tasks, the first of which is to accept the reality of the death and overcome your shock, disbelief, and denial. Many writers, among them Kübler-Ross, believe that seeing the body of the deceased makes this first task easier.

The second task is to struggle through the pain and to identify, accept, and express all of the reactions and feelings that accompany loss without becoming overwhelmed or disabled. At the same time, people must adjust to the concrete changes created by the loss. Coping with the loss of routine, help, and company is the third task. A wife may need to take over the financial matters her husband oversaw and figure out how to handle home maintenance, now that she's on her own. A father needs to reorganize his life without the son who helped him in his business or kept him busy with basketball practice and daily prods to finish homework.

Finally, mourning includes withdrawing energy from your relationship with the deceased, remembering the person in ways that both satisfy your need to connect through good memories and encourage you to move on. This fourth task includes a variety of inner and outer struggles. A husband needs to figure out who he is, now that he's no longer part of a couple, and to restructure his life in ways that respect the loss but still allow him to develop new relationships. A child has to find ways to think of herself as a person who can no longer turn to her mother for advice and comfort but somehow puzzles out new ways to cope with her external world. Loss can require us to revise our identities, our plans, and our dreams, rethinking the meaning of our lives and creating a new framework for living.

How we mourn is structured by community and culture as well as by religion or spiritual practice. It may demand the involvement of a larger, extended family or even an entire clan or tribe. Many cultures restrict the behavior of the bereaved for months, until a second ritual releases them from their duties to the deceased. Some cultures support the development of a narrative about how a person died and who was responsible for it. Even in mainstream culture, stories arise about mistakes that were made or opportunities that were lost ("He should have taken better care of himself"; "She could have lived longer if she'd been diagnosed sooner."). In some cultures, people avoid talking about the deceased altogether.

It may be very important to a bereaved person to follow the customs of his or her culture or to find a way to be free of those norms. When there's diversity within our culture, or within our family, about how mourning should proceed, tensions can erupt in conflict with the people in our lives. Professionals who deal with the dying and bereaved have to understand their cultural context, supporting them in appropriate ways. It's important to respect the cultural worldview and beliefs that are meaningful to a client. Trying to stand outside that framework and manage or prevent the way clients are accustomed to dealing with death can be disruptive, divisive and harmful.

Religion and Spirituality

Religious beliefs and spiritual concerns impact both how people feel about dying and how they react to the loss. Spiritual concerns refer to the construction of meaning in life: finding purpose and attempting to understand how loss can be integrated into your personal narrative. Eric Erickson described the task of integration at some length in his work on the development of adults in the final years of life.

Erickson argued that later adulthood is characterized by a developmental conflict between integrity and despair. Like all of Erickson's stages, this conflict first arises earlier in life; resolving it becomes one's dominant task only at the end. Young people facing a long terminal illness must address this conflict early, as must bereaved people who experience the premature death of a loved one. Integrity requires you to maintain a sense of coherence and wholeness when facing supreme risk, even under the threat of physical, psychological, and social loss. Integrity includes an appreciation of your own life and a timeless love for those who've played a significant role in it.

The virtue born of the conflict between integrity and despair is wisdom, which Erickson defined as informed concern with life, even in the face of death. Failure to achieve integrity arouses disdain, a state of feeling finished, confused, and helpless. Erickson touches here on spirituality as a sense of purpose, competence, love, care, and contribution to society. Grieving people and the dying both find themselves examining all the issues posed by Erickson's final dilemma, whether they've been prepared for this by many years of living or not. Your values and your beliefs about the mysterious shape not just the rituals and customs through which you participate in life but how you experience loss, as well, and, when the time comes, how you'll deal with death.

A 2017 review article by investigators at Oxford University analyzed 100 relevant studies about religion and fear of death. They were primarily interested in two types of religiosity, the degree of a person's intrinsic belief in God and in an afterlife—a strong belief—and the degree of someone's extrinsic religious behavior, making sure they attend their place of worship, genuflect, and pray in order to gain the emotional and social benefits of following a religion—a weak belief. The studies that reported a relationship between fear of death and religiosity concluded that people with strong religious beliefs were less afraid of death. They also found that atheists feared death less than people with weak religious beliefs.

Now, isn't that interesting: the people with the greatest fear were those who were moderately religious, but not fervently so. In fact, there was an inverted U-shaped function between increasing religious conviction, on the x axis, and fear of death, on the y, in studies robust enough to test for such a sophisticated function. Another way of saying this is that fear of death rises as religiosity increases from no belief in God and an afterlife to a weak, uncertain belief, where you might presume there's a final judgment but live life as if there's not. The strength of fear of death falls again as religiosity increases from uncertain beliefs to the type of convictions that compel a true believer to lead a moral, faithful life. The faithful, it seems, feel assured of their salvation.

Non-believers tended to be younger than most religious subjects in these studies. Maybe an ability to distance themselves from thoughts of their own mortality helps to explain both their lower anxiety about dying and, in turn, their disinterest in being saved from it. They'll have the time it takes before they die to redeem themselves.

More than half of the 100 studies reviewed in the Oxford study reported no clear link between death anxiety and the strength of religious beliefs. People who were more religious in these studies didn't seem to be protected from fear by their beliefs, though the authors did point out that non-believers were left out of this group of studies. This finding might be understood by a tendency of extrinsically motivated believers to fear God's judgment, feeling cut off by their wrongdoings, incapable of ever doing enough to be deserving of God's love. A disposition similar to this was found in a Gallup poll published in the late nineties. Gallup reported that more than half of the respondents feared not being worthy of God's forgiveness. Perhaps religious individuals with especially firm, intrinsic beliefs have found a way around this fear of divine judgment and its possibly permanent damnation.

Almost all of the studies reviewed by the Oxford group were conducted in the United States, though a few were drawn from the Middle East and Asia. This makes it difficult to generalize across cultures, but the studies they did include represented data for 26,000 people—quite a number. For more details about this study, you can check out a summary at: http://www.ox.ac.uk/news/2017-03-24-study-who-least-afraid-death.

A report from the National Institute of Health that looked at the first 14 months after a loved one dies, suggested that people with strong religious beliefs resolve their grief more quickly. They also recover more quickly after the death of a child or a spouse, the most disruptive kind of experience. Those with weak or no religious beliefs had more difficulty coming to terms with a death during the first nine months but appeared to recover rapidly after that. No differences in recovery were found for people of different ages, though the data did show that people become more religious with age.

Throughout world history, most people have had access to only one or two religious traditions. Today in America, however, people are free to choose from among a huge variety of religious ideas and traditions, with hundreds, if not thousands, of competing sects, a scenario that encourages people to write their own narratives about death and bereavement. People can choose from Buddhist, Christian, or Islamic rituals. They can mix the symbols of their religious heritage with images from popular culture, poems, and prayers that have served them well in other moments. They can follow examples from their extended families or cultural heroes. Whether these new hybrid forms are helpful or not is anybody's guess. The panoply of choices does, however, reflect the values of choice and autonomy that pervade American culture.

Stages and Styles

There are several well-known frameworks that conceptualize grief as a series of stages. One set of stages was described by John Bowlby, a famous British psychiatrist who developed attachment theory. Bowlby saw grief as an instinctual, adaptive set of responses to loss. He described four phases that trace the course of normal, uncomplicated grief. In the first phase, the bereaved generally feel numb. This is followed by a phase of yearning and searching. Disorganization and despair arise in the next phase, and, then, in stage four, people begin to reorganize their lives. All the urges or emotions that accompany grief, including anxiety, anger, and depression, are part of the reconstruction of one's inner life as it aligns with the new, external reality created by the death.

A similar progression outlined by Robert Cavanaugh in the early seventies parallels Kübler-Ross's stages of dying, beginning with shock and denial. Even when a death is well anticipated, the survivors feel shock and denial at the moment it actually occurs. Denial is not always a dysfunctional response. It can provide a respite and a bit of calm in a life that is suddenly upended by an important loss. It allows us to process overwhelming events a little bit at a time. Denial doesn't necessarily mean that people act as though the death never happened. Denial can simply mean moving in and out of recognition and despair about how completely this event will change everything, biting off only what we can chew in the moment.

Disorganization includes the feeling that one is on autopilot or in a daze. People feel confused and can't make sense out of all the tasks that arise, from decisions about the disposition of the body to what food should be ordered for the gathering after the funeral. Disorganization gives way to feelings of anger and helplessness. Emotions can be intense and may include shame or hatred and jealousy, as the magnitude of the loss penetrates the dazed confusion of survivors. They might lash out at medical caregivers, friends, family, or even people who had nothing to do with the death or the family. Rage at God, or at the deceased, are also common. In many cultures, people wail and tear their clothes. Expressions of fear and rage are acceptable, even encouraged in much of the world. In America, many of us hide or cover our faces, trying to remain calm and look collected. Jackie Kennedy became a cultural icon for her conduct as a widow. She seemed to remain centered and calm, quietly weeping behind the black veil. It's not clear that this is the best way to approach grief, but it's admired by many in the U.S Mainstream America isn't comfortable with emotionality, a reluctance that may bear its own costs.

Stage four in Cavanaugh's scheme is characterized by guilt. The focus of anger shifts from the external world to the self as we look for some one to blame. "If only I had (or hadn't)...," we might think. The social sys tem reinforces this guilt, especially if the death was an accident, a suicide, o a murder. If it were a natural death, but related to lifestyle issues—like diet exercise, or proper self-care—these are often believed to be important fac tors in the death. People want to see death, particularly an untimely death as preventable. Stories that lay blame help people regain a sense of contro over their own mortality.

Guilt is followed by loneliness, sadness, and depression. Attempt to circumvent these kinds of feelings, such as trying to find a new relation ship right away, taking a big expensive vacation, or getting a new pet, usual ly offer only temporary escapes. But we may find there's no way around th loss, only through it. Grief and mourning take time. At some point, though relief arrives. A day goes by where one doesn't think about the deceased o feel miserable and hopeless. At first, feelings of relief can trigger guilt bu little by little, a new life emerges.

Reestablishment is the final phase in Cavanaugh's scheme. Man experts believe that allowing ourselves to fully experience and express a the anxiety, anger, and despair that accompany mourning will free us soone for the task of rebuilding our lives and reinvesting in new relationships People who cannot fully "go there" may find themselves blocked from mov ing forward. Good social support, time, and hope for the future can get u through the worst of it. When people don't have or won't avail themselve of these things, they get stuck and may be unable to fully embrace a re constructed life. A small percentage of people, however, manage grief wel without deep emotional expression. There's not much research on those wh take this route. It may be a lonely path but, for some, it works well enough

In recent years, researchers have focused less on stages or phase and more on differing styles. Men, for example, aren't as expressive of sadness as women are and tend to experience more rage and anger. Women cry more often, and they talk about their losses more than men do. Longitudinal studies of bereavement haven't provided strong support for a stage model, raising questions about whether it's necessary for all mourners to confront and work through a loss. Traditional stage models of grief may underestimate people's ability to adapt to loss and trauma.

New ideas about grief include a dual-process model of coping that frames grief as an oscillation between, on the one hand, confronting the loss and, on the other, compartmentalizing it so that the mourner can attend to the life changes necessitated by the death. In this framework, mourning is viewed as more of a cycle than a linear or stage-like process. Mourners repeatedly revisit the loss and the variety of associated emotions, as they reorganize their relationship to the deceased and take on new roles and responsibilities. Researchers often conceptualize bereavement as an effort at the reconstruction of meaning that cannot be separated from the reactions and beliefs of family and community and the social identity of the mourner. The interpersonal landscape changes when someone dies, and these changes have clear implications for the social network from which people derive approval and support. The work of reconstructing one's world is especially difficult in cases of traumatic death where the inability to make sense of the death can lead to more protracted kinds of grief.

Complicated Grief

Bereavement follows the predictable course when it's openly shared and socially sanctioned, but there are a variety of circumstances where this is not the case. For example, complications arise when your relationship to the deceased isn't recognized by others. This happens to people who've been involved in significant extramarital relationships or in a cohabitation kept under wraps. LBGTQ people often suffer from poor social support for their relationship from family and from the heterosexual people around them, making it difficult to do the work required for normal recovery.

These kinds of problems also arise when a loss is not considered important by others, as may happen when one has an abortion or miscarries, or when an aunt or uncle you're close to dies. Grief counseling may be helpful when the community isn't able to provide support, particularly for an abortion. Abortions often happen in secret and can be terrifying. Grief can come unexpectedly, leaving the survivor no way to express her feelings of anger, guilt, remorse, or loss. The death of a divorced spouse, especially if the ex is the parent of one's children, can be difficult, since the current spouse is usually the focus of concern for the community. The death of a beloved animal can be unexpectedly emotional for many, particularly if it's sudden or if the owner has had to put the animal down.

Sometimes society doesn't recognize the grief of people who are incapacitated or seem less likely to know what's going on, including children and people with cognitive or emotional disabilities. Adolescents may intensely grieve the death of a peer they don't know very well, facing down their own mortality for the first time. Adults can treat these responses as melodramatic, out-of-control, or even silly.

If you're having a hard time accepting a death due to suicide or murder, grief can be isolating and full of rage. Others don't understand what you're going through and don't know how to act around you. You need to talk about the deceased, but all your usual ways of connecting with friends may be blocked along with other normal outlets for your stress. When you're left with ambivalent feelings toward the deceased, anger can be overwhelming, as can guilt. Your depression, isolation, and mixture of guilt and anger can be confusing and difficult, not just for you but for everyone involved.

Death that occurs as a result of warfare or a terrorist attack is a special case of complicated grief. First, it's sudden and violent, two factors that make it especially difficult. Such a death is often accompanied by horrifying images, stark, visual evidence of an event that may have involved mortal danger and physical injury for survivors. Feelings of guilt that you've survived are common, along with overwhelming anger, not only at the enemy or the perpetrator, but at one's own government for its failure to provide security ahead of time or to respond well to victims in the aftermath.

Counseling After a Death

Programs designed to intervene in the lives of the bereaved are often referred to by thanatology as *postvention*. Postvention typically emphasizes the expression of emotions such as guilt, shame, and anger. Survivors are offered empathy and a reassurance that such feelings are normal and, above all, that grief work requires time and patience. But society has little time for death. People too often rush the process in ways that may reduce distress but simultaneously prolong it.

Experiencing intense anger and pain isn't crazy. It's not even abnormal. These feelings are common among people who lose someone who's been present in their lives every day for years. In the first month or two, when you're feeling numb and detached, you may think you're doing pretty well, only to be disappointed when the shock wears off and the pain and anger break through. Programs of postvention help survivors manage intense feelings through journaling or robust physical exercise or even by finding an out-of-the-way place to scream.

These programs recommend sticking to routine, getting out of bed and getting dressed every day, going to work, or getting some exercise. Planning to do something each day is a good strategy in the first three to six months when the hardest part of grieving often occurs. Many people experience setbacks, especially on holidays, birthdays, and anniversaries. It can help to make a list—of projects, books to read, places to go, and friends to call—that can be handy when the walls close in again. Below are some ideas about getting through the holidays in the first year after a loved one's death.

1. Do you want to stay home or run away to someplace entirely different? It's OK to want to get away if it helps.
2. What kind of changes might make the holidays easier? Is it possible to let someone do some of the tasks you usually do yourself? Don't be stuck in a holiday routine for the sake of others.
3. What gifts will you need to purchase? Make a list well in advance, so you can get the shopping done on your "good days."
4. Is there a memorial that might seem appropriate? Planting a

garden, having a short ceremony, or organizing a memorial fundraiser can give you something to focus on and provide an opportunity for friends and family to participate and offer support.

5. Do you just want to be alone? Being by yourself is a legitimate choice.

Source: Costa, B.J. (1989). *Handbook for the bereaved and those who want to help.* Fall River, MA: Hospice Outreach.

For most people, bereavement runs its course in nine to 12 months. Survivors may, however, continue to experience moments of loneliness and distress for years, especially after the death of a child.

In the *Handbook of Thanatology*, the authors remind us that grief and bereavement don't take place in a vacuum. Intervention should include an assessment of cultural factors, economic and emotional resources, spiritual beliefs, as well as race, gender, ethnicity, structural inequality, and social class. It's important to remember that the meaning of death can differ substantially from one person to the next, one family to the next, and one community to the next.

Appreciative inquiry focuses on survivors' accounts of their own feelings and experience rather than on an attempt to force them through phases or make them try strategies that seem strange or meaningless. Interventions need to honor the original responses to death and grief that arise from the unique circumstances in a particular individual's life, responses that are shaped by that person's relationship to the deceased. Counseling must adapt to specific social and economic environments, exploring what matters most for each survivor and each family. Bereavement counseling should take a collaborative, exploratory approach that permits respectful communication and ongoing learning on both sides of the partnership.

The *Handbook of Thanatology* also acknowledges the importance of the role of spirituality in a holistic approach to death. Religious or spiritual ideas and beliefs can help people find meaning and personal growth

hrough suffering. Visits from clergy, chaplains, and other spiritual counsel-
rs can be helpful. Faith communities can offer comfort and support as well
s tangible assistance with everyday tasks. Prayer and meditation can give
urvivors something tangible to do to ease their stress.

The *Handbook* also offers a list of symptoms that might be useful
1 assessing whether a person is experiencing a particularly complicated
rocess. These symptoms include trouble accepting the death or protracted
eelings of numbness and detachment that persist after the first six months.
n inability, by the end of the first year, to trust others, make new friends,
r pursue new interests is also on the *Handbook's* list, along with excessive
itterness and anger or feeling that life's been rendered meaningless.

Disturbances in social and occupational activities or chronic, dis-
uptive feelings of longing and yearning for the deceased can also be prob-
ematic, especially if they're acutely persisting after the first six months.
'omplicated grief is often accompanied by intense distress, physical illness,
nd social dysfunction. Deaths that were unexpected or violent, a previous
istory of loss and trauma, and poor social-support systems make it all the
ore likely that survivors will experience a difficult recovery.

Hospices, funeral homes, churches, hospitals, and social service
gencies offer a wide variety of support, including information, bereavement
roups, and professional counseling. These programs may include storytell-
g, journaling, music and other expressive arts, meditation, and bodywork.
here's little research that evaluates the efficacy of various intervention
pproaches. What evidence there is suggests that formal interventions are
ost effective in complicated bereavement. Almost everyone in the world
as experienced or will experience bereavement, and almost everyone in the
orld will eventually get through it and reconstruct a new life. But getting
rough and moving on doesn't mean forgetting the deceased. In fact, the
emory of the deceased may be used to lay the foundation for rebuilding a
warding life, different from the old one but integrated with its strengths.

References for This Chapter:

James, J. W., & Friedman, R. (2009). *The grief recovery handbook* (20th Anniversary, expanded ed.). New York, NY: Harper Collins.

PDQ Supportive and Palliative Care Editorial Board. (April 20 2017). Grief, Bereavement, and Coping with Loss (PDQ®). Retrieved from PubMed Health, https://www.ncbi.nlm.nih.gov/pubmedhealth PMH0032576/

CHAPTER 15

SENSING OTHER DIMENSIONS:
NEAR DEATH EXPERIENCES

Death is a final doorway into the unknown. Because we're not able to study the experience of the moment of death and don't know what lies behind that impenetrable door, a *near-death experience* (NDE) may offer a glimpse into the possibility of a some kind of continuation after death. The phenomenon of near death happens when a person dies for a short duration and is then revived. During this brief interval, a person can step into an intense but often joyful experience of a transcendental existence that can be at once confusing, scary, and inspiring. When adults or children experience a NDE, it changes what they think and how they feel about life and death.

Near death is a difficult topic to research. First, the experience isn't tangible. In fact, it takes place outside our corporeal body altogether. Second, NDEs occur outside our familiar surroundings, in some unknown dimension. Third, people have trouble describing what happened because whatever they saw, heard, and possibly understood at the time exists outside our known world. Finally, a NDE is a subjective experience permeated by a variety of cultural and religious frames of reference. How then do we study an event that's so subjective and indescribable? What tools do we use to measure a transcendental phenomenon that's not within the concrete parameters of our universe? These are but a few of the challenges that scientists face as they research the topic.

Although stories of NDE are unique to the individual, the descriptions do share common features. In particular, adults come to believe that life continues after death on a different plane. There's a clear awareness of an inner self or spirit that's very much a continuation of who we are as individuals, an essence of our individuality that exists after death. For children, a spiritual life not necessarily in accord with their culture or country of origin often develops after the experience. Where and how near-death experience occurs is a mystery, yet the phenomenon occurs regularly for people of all ages, with many observable similarities.

The term near-death experience was coined in 1975 by the psychiatrist Raymond Moody in his book, *Life after Life*. Before this term was established, Russell Noyes described it as a mystical consciousness. Near death is not a new experience but an ancient phenomenon that has been found in the literature from Europe, the Middle East, Africa, India, and other places. Plato in *The Republic* tells us of a soldier named Er who died in battle but then returned to life to describe his visit into another world. Similarly, the Lazarus phenomenon, or Lazarus complex, is a medical term used when people spontaneously revive after they were pronounced dead due to a delayed, spontaneous return of circulation after cardiac arrest. The term was taken from the biblical story of Lazarus, who was resurrected by Christ four days after his death. It is estimated that a third of people who die and come back to life have a near-death experience.

Near death was and continues to be of major interest to physicians, psychiatrists, and researchers from different disciplines, including nurses, social workers, and chaplains. Many in the field study the phenomenon empirically in order to understand how to help people face the psychological, emotional, and spiritual impact of NDE. Although death may be the longest-standing mystery, researchers have developed standards and tools to study the experience of near-death. Nevertheless, one of the challenges in incorporating the near-death experience into daily life is that often doctors and families don't consider that NDE is real.

It is important to note that the study of NDE has not been accepted by many scientific circles. Conducting empirical research is therefore important. Empirical research is an investigation relying on observed and measured phenomena. Typical characteristics include (a) a specific research question; (b) definitions of the population and of the behavior or the phenomenon being studied; and (c) a description of the research method (the process followed in the study), including the design and the testing instruments used. Often, reports of empirical research include statistical analysis of the data and a discussion of the implications of the findings.

New Research on NDEs

Scientific research into NDE continues to improve, benefitting from systematic follow-up of large groups of participants and from advancing technology with more sophisticated measurement and data gathering. Empirical research designs have created new scientific norms for studying NDE. Beginning in 1980, a psychologist by the name of Kenneth Ring developed the Weighted Core Experience Index (WCEI), a 10-point interview scale that assesses and standardizes the analysis of near-death experiences. A few years later, in 1983, the psychiatrist Bruce Greyson developed the Near-Death Experience Scale. This instrument differentiates between people who've unequivocally claimed to have had a NDE and those with qualified or questionable claims. Both tools have improved the consistency of research in a field that was dominated by retrospective studies and analyses.

For example, a group of scientists from the Netherlands researched the near-death phenomenon with 344 cardiac patients. Using the Ring and the Greyson scales, the researchers further defined NDE as a reported memory of an extraordinary state of consciousness, including out-of-body experience, pleasant feelings, going through a tunnel, and seeing and communicating with a light. In NDEs, people also report being with deceased family members or conducting a life review. *Clinical death*—the time during which the NDE occurs—was defined by this group as a period of unconsciousness caused by inadequate blood supply to the brain, cessation of breathing, or both.

The Netherlands team conducted their research with patients who were resuscitated in coronary care units in 10 Dutch hospitals. This means that the patients were considered clinically dead for a period of several minutes before they were revived. If a patient is not resuscitated within five to 10 minutes, there is a greater possibility of permanent damage to the brain, including death. Of the 344 patients, 62 (18%) reported a NDE.

The first interview cycle took place within a few days of resuscitation. Using Ring's WCEI scale, the researchers categorized NDE into three types of experiences: superficial; core; and deep. Superficial experiences were included because, in the follow-up interviews, people reported transformational changes similar to those in the other two categories. The research team continued to follow up with interviews at two and eight years after the resuscitation. The interviews included a life-change inventory and both medical and psychological evaluations.

The 344 patients had undergone 509 successful resuscitations, which means that some patients experienced clinical death more than once; some of these had more than one NDE. The patients reported many of the elements in the scale, such as being aware of being dead, experiences of positive emotions (joy, peace), feeling as though they were going through a tunnel, and communicating with a light. They reported vivid colors, celestial landscapes, meeting with deceased persons, and having a life review. The follow-up interviews showed a remarkable recall of the near-death experience as well as positive life changes. The patients felt more self-assured and reported that they no longer feared death.

In 2018, an Italian team of researchers published an article on developing an Italian-language version of Greyson's NDE Scale to investigate the frequency and causes of NDE in Italy, especially among patients who'd recovered from coma without residual cognitive impairments or brain damage. The researchers successfully validated the Italian version of Greyson's Scale, a step that could be replicated worldwide in order to universalize a standard measurement tool.

The Italian researchers emphasized that, in addition to the unique aspects of each person's near-death experience, there were similarities, shared elements, and common features that characterize the accumulated studies up to this point. Experiences that were overwhelmingly positive have been life changing, but what about the negative experiences? What do they have in common? What does it mean to have a distressing NDE?

Positive, Negative, and Mixed Near-Death Experiences

Major, hospital-based studies from the U.S., Italy, the UK, and the Netherlands found only positive near-death experiences, including astounding feelings of complete peace and joy. Cardiologist Michael Sabom reported that his large hospital study included very few cases of negative experiences, most of which were perceived to be negative only for a short duration. *Distressing NDEs* do happen, however, and more often than many researchers anticipated. A distressing NDE may include entering a purposeless, meaningless existence within an eternal void. One review reported that 23% of experiences of near-death were disturbing, terrifying, or despairing, with a small percentage even describing the experience as hellish. A *mixed near-death experience* includes both the positive and the negative, typically starting with an unpleasant feeling that then turns into joy.

Across the globe over the next 12 months, there will be hundreds of thousands of reports of near-death experiences. Currently, we have no way of predicting who among them will experience this phenomenon as pleasant, unpleasant, or mixed. Each of these three groups consists of people with a variety of personal attributes, including demographic variables. Individuals who have had distressing NDEs have been unfairly judged, as if there must be valid reasons their experience was negative. To the contrary, there's no evidence that this group can be distinguished by their beliefs, by how they've led their lives, or by any other qualities, traits, or characteristics.

Nancy Evans Bush has researched near-death experiences for many years after experiencing a shockingly distressing NDE during childbirth. In her book, *Dancing Past the Dark*, she used the language of science to trace the historical progress of studying NDEs, quantifying and measuring not only positive or distressing experiences, but also the aftereffects of near death. Bush believes that the yearning for a positive existence after death may have overshadowed the research on reports of distressing NDEs. While some large studies showed no negative experiences, there are small collections of darker experiences that have varied and unique features. These negative experiences do, however, share some common patterns that have been revealed by Ring's and Greyson's scales.

A nine-year study by Bush and Greyson, published in 1993 in the journal *Psychiatry*, measured 50 distressing NDEs. Three different types of descriptions emerged. The first one showed that some NDEs judged as positive were actually experienced as terrifying. The second type was being utterly alone in a world described as a featureless void. The third type, reported least often, was an experience of despair in a hellish, endlessly evil place.

People respond differently to a distressing NDE. Bush and Greyson have described three typical responses: (a) deciding to turn one's life around and become a positive influencer; (b) dismissing the experience as meaningless brain activity; and (c) beginning a long-haul effort at integration as one struggles to make sense of the experience.

Children—who seem to have a higher percentage of NDEs compared to adults—also experience them as positive, mixed, and distressing. Any type of NDE is puzzling, even to adults. Children, however, are more likely to find the experience to be overwhelming and to describe it as negative, disregarding its positive components. Both adults and children find it helpful when someone carefully listens to their stories. Given that it's more difficult for children to express their feelings or describe unfamiliar surroundings, validation of their experience is especially important for the continued healthy development of a child.

"Bad" people don't inevitably have distressing or negative near-death experiences, while "good" people don't automatically experience joy. In fact, studies show that prisoners who are incarcerated for murder report positive and uplifting NDEs. On the other hand, as early as 1565, Teresa of Avila pointedly observed that even saints can endure horrific spiritual journeys, sojourning in hell. Her own illness-prompted vision of being taken to hell depicts many of the NDE features found in Ring's and Greyson's scales such as going through a dark, narrow passage (a tunnel), spirits that looked evil, and confinement in a cupboard (the void). Six years after the event, Teresa of Avila still remembered exactly what had happened and continued to be affected by the ecstasy and insights she experienced. Such constructive aftereffects are also typical of NDEs, both positive and negative.

Many other famous spiritual figures have had near-death or spiritual experiences and visions incorporating various NDE features, with positively life-changing effects. King David described a walk through the valley of death. The Christian gospel documents three days that Jesus spent in hell between his death and resurrection. Buddha is depicted meditating with serpents and demons surrounding him. Good and bad may appear within the same experience, but what seems to matter is that the individual in the middle of this chaos embraces life's worthy choices. As Teresa of Avila wrote, momentary darkness accentuates the immense brightness of the light. It was the defining lesson of her life.

Whether the near-death experiences of people were positive, negative, or mixed and regardless of their age, follow up studies continue to show that people who work on integrating the experience into their lives have exceptionally positive aftereffects. Nancy Bush's story and the stories of Buddha, Jesus, and Teresa of Avila suggest that good and bad are interwoven elements of existence and that the world here on earth and the one beyond are somehow interconnected, perhaps even unified in a whole.

NDE Changes How We View and Live Our Lives

Much of the interpretation of a NDE is dependent on the person's cultural upbringing, language, religion, and belief system. Descriptions of the experience are shaped by differing preexisting world views. But two specific universal NDE patterns bind many cultures together. The first one is the feeling of acceptance that surrounds people while in the state of near-death and a sense of a growing love and compassion for all human beings. The second is a journey from horrific sufferings to resurrection, from a bad or even a hellish experience to a spiritual integration. Whether the experience is good or bad, involving bliss or suffering, people who've had a NDE are likely to develop a new awareness of a universal connectedness or *holism*.

Holism can be seen through many cultural lenses. In both Western and Eastern traditions, the theory of holism holds that parts of the whole are interconnected and cannot exist independently of the whole. We better understand the parts when we understand the whole. But we also understand that the whole is greater than the sum of its parts. A Buddhist may call this enlightenment. Taoism views it as the integration of yin and yang: light is part of the dark, and darkness is part of light. A Native American shaman or medicine woman may describe it as the universal power of wisdom.

In *The Republic*, Er described his journey as transformative. The Sufi master Rumi called it the way of the heart. Jesus framed holism as God's eternal love, knowing and caring for each and every human being. Jesus's idea of universal love was spiritual yet also practical in that it encourages us to love our neighbors as ourselves. In the eighteenth century, Immanuel Kant considered enlightenment not as a personal journey but as collective progress toward the epitome of human development, a maturity that endows human beings with reason and justice. The end result of growing into enlightenment is the achievement of universal peace.

Famous historical figures or saints aren't alone in these realizations. The aftereffects of near-death have led many individuals, both adults and children, into spiritual contemplations and the development of greater love and compassion towards others.

Is the Near Death Experience Real or Imagined?

Researchers are divided about the cause and nature of NDE. Is it a reality outside our physical world or a product of our imagination? Two theoretical views epitomize this argument: the "biological/psychological" and the "survivalist" camps have emerged. The first camp, from cognitive neuroscience, views the experience as a manifestation of normal brain function that's gone awry, due to neurochemical changes in a dying brain or one that's stressed during a traumatic, life-threatening event. Either way, on this side of the argument, the brain manufactures certain chemicals that create visions and feelings that are experienced as real but are hallucinatory in nature.

The second theoretical view frames the mind and body as separate, with an inner selfhood or soul that survives after the body dies. Memories, self-identity, and even emotions continue on after your physical death. This group of researchers takes into consideration the occurrence of experiences similar to near-death among people who haven't experienced life-threatening events. These experiences or visions can't be explained by biological or psychological responses to either clinical death or the threat of death.

In 2014, in order to ascertain whether the brain is involved in manufacturing NDE memories, a group of scientists from the University of Padova, Italy, designed a study to test how the brain responds and stores memories of near-death experiences. The team discovered that regular memories and NDE memories are linked to the same electroencephalographic (EEG) patterns. They concluded that NDE memories cannot be linked to some imagined visions because they are stored in the brain alongside memories of concrete events. In other words, the brain itself thinks and treats NDE memories as real.

Similarly, a European-funded research project in Belgium worked with three groups of coma survivors to compare the phenomenological characteristics of NDEs with other memories of real and imagined events. Phenomenological characteristics include perceptions (visual, auditory, olfactory, tactile), spatial and temporal features (space and time), and emotional information (joy, fear, and so on). First, the team discovered that imagined events have fewer phenomenological characteristics than real events, and, second, they found that the physiological origins and characteristics of NDE memories are the same as real-life memories. NDEs were found to be as real as other life events even though the experience itself didn't take place in the known, material world. This contrast begs the long-asked questions scientists find difficult to answer: Who are we? Are human beings more than a collection of cells? Does consciousness exist outside the brain?

NDEs and Consciousness

The argument over the origin of NDEs isn't confined to the question of whether it's real or hallucinatory. As Dr. Eben Alexander, III, explains, the presumption that somehow our complex brains create our consciousness has not been proven. There are no conclusive studies that our brain is the center of our personality or consciousness. Since neurons alone don't give rise to personhood, scientists inevitably arrive at what David Chalmers coined "the hard problem of consciousness." Does consciousness exist because the brain manifests or produces it as a physical process, or does consciousness exist independently of the embodied brain?

To date, we have no fundamental explanation for the origin of our consciousness. No matter how much scientists try to attach the brain to the creation of this identity that we each recognize as "me," there are no convincing data. The brain with all of its intricacy doesn't create consciousness. As it stands, many experts in quantum mechanics, including Albert Einstein, have unexpectedly found themselves at the door of mysticism as they tried to explain the existence of consciousness.

Ongoing research inquiries, along with the data that physicians nurses, and chaplains collect as they treat patients, keep removing bricks from the wall that's been erected between science and spirituality. Many researchers and healthcare providers doubt that near-death experiences are due somehow to hallucinations or a last-minute gasp of a dying brain. NDEs are transformative events for those who've experienced them because of the realness of the phenomenon itself. The experience of a foreign universe outside the limitations of our known physicality may be alarming, but it also serves to challenge our previous assumptions and even our imagination.

An article by a group of scientists and nurses, in the journal *International Emergency Nursing*, pointed out that if NDEs are due to faulty brain function, the phenomenon would occur in all patients who are critically ill and near death. Furthermore, laboratory-based research has concluded that in NDEs the mind can separate from the body or transcend the physical boundaries of the body. These experiments show that the different features of NDEs, such as going through a tunnel or being outside of one's body, do not necessarily happen only when people are clinically dead. Studies like those of Dean Radin, of the Institute of Noetic Sciences, contribute additional weight to the view that near-death may be a genuine experience.

But do NDEs mean that there's life after death? Some argue that even if the phenomenon of NDE occurs outside the body, the experience doesn't necessarily lead to the assumption that life continues after death. Christopher Moreman has emphasized that no matter what powerful effects an NDE has on the individual, the experience in itself doesn't provide hard evidence for an afterlife. That said, the sum total of studies on death and dying, including research on other extraordinary phenomena, do not allow us to easily close the case on the possibility of life after death.

Even though the phenomenon of NDE often defies words, the *unity thesis*, the feeling of unity between self and cosmos, may be a clue for life beyond the physical world. Ralf W. Wood explains William James's unity thesis, the *eternal unanimity*, as a common core of the experience of mysticism. Human beings all over the world have many beliefs and views, but the experiences of extraordinary phenomena have a unifying thesis.

In research, we can see this unifying thesis through thematic analysis studies such as one from the recent collaboration of the University of Liège and the University Hospital of Liège, Belgium. Rich and meticulous, the study described the common core experiences of NDEs. Thematic analysis of in-depth interviews with 34 cardiac-arrest survivors extracted ten *time-bounded themes* and one *transversal theme*. Time-bounded themes are isolated events encountered during the near-death time frame, such as going through a tunnel, seeing a light, and encountering other beings. The one transversal theme emerged as people reflected back on the whole experience. They all reported an altered perception of time, as though time didn't exist. It may well be that this unified experience of unconfined time is as close as we come to the experience of eternity.

Children's descriptions of near-death experiences are similar to adults' unifying experiences. Often, children have reported that they were accompanied in their NDE by a being who held their hand as they passed through a tunnel and into the light. Key findings in the studies of children and NDE show that acknowledgement by their physician that their experience was real helped them to constructively integrate the experience into their lives. In contrast, some children whose experiences were not validated fell into depression.

In the quest to understand near-death experiences, one thing remains constant. No matter where we are in the world and what religion or belief system we hold, NDE is a shared, unifying commonality. Honoring the experience and the experiencer is essential. The advice offered by John C. Hagan, III, in his book, *The Science of Near Death Experience*, seems wise: whether physicians believe or disbelieve in the reality of NDE, they need to acknowledge that the phenomenon occurred to their patients, regardless of age, and learn how to care for those who have experienced it.

References for This Chapter:

Greyson, B., Kelly, E. W., Kelly, E. F. (2009). Explanatory models for near-death experiences. In: Holden, J. M., Greyson, B., James, D. (Eds.), *The handbook of near-death experiences*. Santa Barbara, CA Praeger Publishers, pp. 213-234.

Hagan, J. C. (2017). *The science of near-death experiences*. Columbia, MO: University of Missouri Press.

Holden, J. M., Greyson, B. E, James, D. E. (2009). *The handbook of near-death experiences: Thirty years of investigation*. Santa Barbara, CA Praeger Publishers, pp. 63-86.

Martial, C., Cassol, H. Antonopoulos, G., Charlier, T., Heros, J. Donneau, A.F., ... & Laureys, S. (2017). Temporality of features in near-death experience narratives. *Frontiers in human neuroscience, 11*, 311.

Moody R. (1975). *Life After Life*. New York, NY: Bantam Books.

Moreman, C. M. (2018). *Beyond the threshold: Afterlife beliefs and experiences in world religions*. Lanham, MD: Rowman & Littlefield.

Ring, K. (1980). *Life at death: A scientific investigation of the near death experience*. New York: Coward, McCann & Geoghegan.

Sabom, M. B. (1982). *Recollections of death: A medical investigation*. New York, NY: Harper and Row.

CHAPTER 16

GOING FORWARD: RENEWAL AND REVITALIZATION

There is no one best way to die or to grieve, just as there is no one best way to live. Meaning and beauty can be communicated in acceptance and grace, in resistance, or even in defiance. We are inspired by those who go through life's trials with equanimity, but no less so by those who "rage against the dying of the light," as Dylan Thomas once wrote in a poem for his dying father.

Dying and grieving are human affairs, as well as biological events. Each has a moral, spiritual, and ethical dimension, and the acceptance of mortality keeps one in touch with nature and with one's own effort to make a difference in the world. Think about what life would be like without death. Family, love, work, and all of the important human realities, including the experience of time itself, would be dramatically altered. Humans would live quite differently if life were not finite and time limited.

Seeing death up close can make us more aware of what it means to be alive. It adds urgency to our existence. Those who cannot face death may shut out much of life. They back away from friends who are dying, from those who are bereaved, and from those who take care of the dying. People who are unwilling to deal with death also lose a sense of wholeness by denying a central human experience. They may respond to dying, and to their own mortality, in strange and mechanical ways that restrain sensitivity and imagination. As one of the founders of death education wrote,

Education relates not only to death itself but to our feelings about ourselves in nature and the universe we live in. It has to do with values and ideals, the way we relate to one another and the kind of world we are building. Thoughtfully pursued, it can deepen the quality of our lives and of our relationships John D. Morgan (1987), p. 183.

Coming face to face with death can invigorate. It snaps us out of day-to-day irritations and our boredom with the mundane, reminding us that we have only so much time. It can energize our plans and decisions about the milestones of life—marriage, career, family, and mortality. Over and over again, dying people have affirmed the impact of encountering mortality by throwing themselves into life. Contact with the dying can serve as a deep source of courage for the survivors and a wellspring for action, propelling us toward a more meaningful, integrated life. It can sharpen our values, priorities, and goals. It can help us to savor small blessings—the sweetness of a pear or the playfulness of a puppy.

The study of death prepares us to deal with the anger, shock, guilt, and sadness we're likely to feel when confronted by death. Dying frees everyone to take risks and be creative in a way not possible when limited by fearing all the risks in life. It can offer opportunities for psychological and spiritual healing and for unconditional love. It seems essential that we engage in this encounter, particularly as we move into a historical period in which so many elderly people will die at the end of long illnesses that are accompanied by grave disabilities. We're likely to face a *bereavement overload*, and the longer we live the more likely this is.

Our sisters and brothers, our friends and acquaintances, the heroes of our youth, and the famous people we know will all die one day, many of them before we do. The impact of any death, of course, varies not only with the survivor but with the survivor's relationship to the dying person. Facing all of this can distress us, but it also teach us how to cope with adversity, to find joy in life, and to better support those around us.

Relationship and Death

The death of an elderly parent is a normative experience in adult life. Adult children anticipate their parents' deaths, as a father or mother becomes frailer and exhibits a cognitive and physical decline while an illness becomes progressively debilitating. As grown sons and daughters age, they may exhibit adaptation anxiety, worrying about how they will provide for the parent or how they will react to the parent's death. It's unclear whether or not adaption anxiety makes any difference in bereavement, but complicated grief following the death of a parent is rare, most often occurring only when the relationship with the parent was conflicted or immature.

By age 54, 50% of all adults have lost both parents, usually losing their fathers first. The death of a parent can have profound effects on sibling relationships—good relationships often become better, and bad ones become worse. The death of the second parent changes the family's organization, breaking up some families and drawing others together. Facing the fact that "people in this family die, too," can lead to a new level of maturity in middle age.

The death of a spouse is always a life-altering event. Things often change dramatically when a spouse dies, especially if it's unexpected. One loses a helpmate, a lover, often a best friend (this is especially true for men) and, if there are children involved, a co-parent. Your standard of living may change along with your status in your social network. Widowhood means taking over the tasks of the spouse and finding new sources of social and emotional support. Elderly people who are widowed are likely to experience high levels of depression, strong feelings of loneliness, and declines in overall physical and emotional health. Most widowed people, however, show resilience and marked improvement in both social functioning and health by the end of the second or third year following the loss.

Widows

Women are frequently impoverished by the death of a spouse and tend to rely more on their children for emotional, social, and financial support. This new dependence can cause family conflicts and generate negative feelings. Middle-class women have the resources associated with better adjustment, but they still have to cope with the loss of friends and activities that are organized around couples. Widows can make good adjustments, however, at all socioeconomic levels. One classic study outlined three common adaptive styles. *The self-initiating* widow moved away from couple friends, either taking over, reassigning, or giving up her husband's roles, and she often entered into stronger engagement with her community. Widows from traditional cultures who'd lived in gender-segregated communities became immersed in their families, their peer groups, and their neighborhood relationships. Their lives were much less disrupted by the loss of a husband than women who'd spent their lives in a couple-oriented world.

Surprisingly, the third adaptive style was found among isolated, downwardly mobile women, who were unable to maintain the relationships and activities they'd developed in married life. They tended to withdraw from friends and family and seemed fearful of the outside world. They possessed few skills and little confidence. Paradoxically, these women adjusted well, perhaps because they already had such low expectations of life and society. The low economic status of a widow was consistent with her expectations for achieving a satisfying life.

Widowers

Widowers seem to have a more difficult time than widows, perhaps because they are less likely to seek help and have more difficulty establishing new intimate relationships. Generally, widowers had, more often than widows, seen their spouses as their best friends, and they often felt that their wives had been the only people who'd really understood them. Fewer men are widowed than women, and men are usually widowed later than women. Most women realize that they'll probably live longer than their spouses, especially if their husbands were years older. Women, more than men, are psychologically open and emotionally prepared for the loss of a spouse. The worst problem for many women is that their socioeconomic status often plummets, and they can't support the lifestyle they had when their husband was alive.

The problems are different for men. Men are often estranged from their families and have fewer friends than women do. Moreover, they may lack the social skills to build new relationships. Widowers report less anxiety but more loneliness than widows of the same age. For men, the mundane tasks of housekeeping, shopping, and cooking can be formidable, especially if their marriage was structured by traditional gender roles. A man's upbringing may make it more difficult to recognize and express his feelings to others, especially if his wife was the primary confidant in his life.

Two areas of widowhood remain relatively unexplored by researchers. The first is widowhood among gay or lesbian couples. What research there is suggests that widowhood is just as difficult in same-sex couples, and it's often complicated by lack of family support and homophobic or insensitive reactions to their mourning. Like most men, gay men express anger more often and more intensely than lesbians. Community support is especially important for gay or lesbian widows and widowers, who often benefit from gay-bereavement groups and programs specifically designed for bereaved LGBTQ people.

Another gap exists in research about those who feel relieved by the death of a spouse. This reaction is not uncommon among people who've cared for a partner over a long, terminal phase. It may also arise for those who were involved in difficult, unrewarding relationships. A widowed person may view a partner's death as a release from a confining or oppressive partner. Death may also be a relief as it represents the end of suffering for a loved one who'd been extremely ill for a long time. Shame and guilt are common responses to this feeling of relief, despite the fact that it may be perfectly reasonable.

Many writers and researchers maintain that the loss of a child is the hardest of all bereavements. It is never considered normal for a child to die before a parent. This loss rips away the future, the dreams parents held, and the plans they had, and it deprives them of the deep emotional connection with the child, bonds that may have been even stronger than those in the marriage. A child's death can also be seen as a failure of the parent's job to protect and care for the child. Later in life, an elderly parent may feel loss of support and security with the loss of an adult child.

Miscarriages and stillborn babies may evoke complicated grief when the loss is not respected properly and family support is unforthcoming. The death of an infant can be accompanied by overwhelming anxiety and feelings of helplessness, as parents watch the baby struggle in a hospital and are called upon to make heart-wrenching decisions. Parents not only lose the actual relationship with the child but also the meaning and purpose for their lives, that is, to help the child become what they could have become. A long childhood illness punctuated by periods of recovery can be especially difficult for families, as hope alternates with anxiety and despair. It is devastating to be close to a child who can't be saved.

Children and Death

Dying children usually understand that something is terribly wrong, and they can become angry and depressed if they can't talk about their experience. They fear pain, separation, and loss of control over their bodily functions. The entire family becomes highly stressed; siblings often feel anger, jealousy, and guilt. Parents have to set reasonable limits for everyone while they themselves are falling apart. Parents with dying children also tend to withdraw from friends and families who have healthy children. Other parents can feel awkward bringing their children over or even talking about them.

The death of a sibling when one is a child can be extremely difficult, regardless of the cause. Children often take too much responsibility for negative events, wondering if somehow they were at fault. Parents can be unavailable to help surviving children when they're swamped by their own grief over the loss of a child. The death of a parent can also have serious long-term effects on a young child. Not only does the child lose a parent but the other parent can become lost in his or her own bereavement, as well. Intense anger toward the dead parent is common. Young adults who've experienced such a loss are more likely to become depressed. One study found that half of all suicides among college students were those who, as a child, had experienced the death of a parent. The quality of parenting by the surviving parent is critical to the recovery of a child. Children who feel safe and secure in the extended family and those who have an effective surviving parent are less likely to suffer long-term negative effects.

Bereaved children who are able to remain in the same location, go to the same school, and stay in their existing social networks do best. Stability, continuity, and cohesion are important at every level of family functioning, from cooking and housekeeping to communication and continual support from the outside. Telling children the truth about the death of a parent or sibling, and keeping them well-informed throughout the process, is considered a best practice. Children need to be given the opportunity to struggle with change without having to edit their thoughts and stifle their feelings.

Post-traumatic Growth

Major life challenges can lead us to realize that the world is a dangerous place and to highlight our own vulnerability. Positive psychology, a relatively recent theory of behavior change, has led to promising evidence that suffering and loss can be accompanied by positive change and personal growth. Over the past 15 or 20 years, work on resilience and thriving in response to challenge has shown that positive growth has been reported in several domains: personal strength; relating to others; appreciation of life; and spiritual development. Coping with trauma can help us develop a sense that we've been tested and we've survived, that we're courageous and strong and able to deal with whatever life dishes out.

Living through difficult times can also change how we see other people. We can become more committed to others and more compassionate about their suffering. It can bring a greater sense of intimacy and a greater freedom to express all the facets of the self. Traumatic events clearly challenge our philosophy of life, changing our priorities and increasing our appreciation of even the smallest of joys. The intrinsic rewards found in being with other people and spending time with family acquire much greater significance. Extrinsic rewards, such as making money or climbing the corporate ladder lose their luster.

In the United States, some people experience a loss of meaning after trauma, losing faith and suffering from despair, but this response is not predominant. People often report that, after a trauma, their lives are fuller, richer, and more purposeful, although this doesn't automatically translate into feelings of happiness and well-being. Finding meaning in life, even thriving after a trauma, isn't the same thing as finding happiness.

Post-traumatic growth is defined as transformational learning that takes one above and beyond their prior level of functioning. It is different from resilience in that resilience refers to the ability to bounce back to one's prior level of functioning. Some people are able to make strides in their emotional development after facing great adversity. Some are not. For instance, young adults who experience invasive treatments or treatments with greater side effects (such as chemo), especially on a long-term basis, may not experience post-traumatic growth.

Those who thrive also tend to have common characteristics. They tend to be optimistic, open-minded, and extroverted. They have supportive social networks that help them create a narrative about the meaning of traumatic events and their impact on the self. In general, research shows that most people are more resilient than expected. Only about 5% to 10% of people who experience personal trauma, from the death of a loved one to being a victim of crime or disaster, develop long-term mental health problems that cause them to seek the care of mental health professionals. *Posttraumatic growth* has been demonstrated among survivors of serious illness, bereavement, sexual assault, military combat, and terrorist attacks.

Posttraumatic growth takes time. Most research suggests that it's unlikely to be measurable until at least two years after a traumatic event. At that point, people feel competent again, having discovered hidden abilities and strengths. They report greater self-insight and warmer relationships. They often build a new life based on changes in their values and priorities. People from minority backgrounds are even more likely to see benefits, perhaps because of their pre-trauma experience with adversity.

We can't avoid dying eventually, but we can make decisions now that will ensure the best possible conditions for the end of our lives. We can write a will, plan our funeral, and organize our estate so that, when some thing happens to us, our family faces as little stress and confusion as possible. We can't avoid death, but we can face it with courage, wonder, and grit. We can use the inevitability of death to strengthen our bonds to each other and deepen our appreciation of life. We can learn to tolerate sorrow and suffering, to find new purpose, and to focus on what is meaningful. Preparation and pluck can allow us to live our lives fully to the very end.

Conclusion

In this book, we have tried to take you from the first thoughts about death as a child or an adolescent, to the final stages of life. It is our hope that you will find the answers to your questions about living and dying well within its pages and that it will inspire you to begin a conversation with your friends and family that will both educate them about the choices you have made and the ones that are available to them. We hope that it will motivate you to invest the time in advanced care planning, talk to your doctor about your wishes, and ensure that any facilities will utilize, from emergency teams to long-term care, the right information about how you want to live out your life.

If you are the friend or caretaker of a person who is living with a terminal disease, we hope that you find the research here helpful in fulfilling your role, maintaining your well-begin, and coping with the day-to-day challenges that face caregivers all over the world. The opportunity to walk with someone down the last part of their journey is an important experience in life. It isn't easy, and we don't always have the right instincts about what to say or do, but it can teach us to stay open to life in a new way, to stay present in the moment, and to express our feelings toward those we love more freely.

As the baby boomers move toward end-of-life choices, and are likely to overwhelm the current system of care, and the business of death and dying, we believe that it is critical for all of us to accept more responsibility for the care of those who are mortally ill. We will all need to depend on each other for comfort and strength. When 10,000 people a day die, if each of them has 10 close family members and friends, 100,000 people will be strongly affected by a death each day. That means, that within a year, 36,500,000 people will be affected by the death of someone close. The numbers are stunning. If you are a member of the baby boom generation, a child of the baby boom generation, or a friend of a baby boomer (that would include almost everyone), you may find yourself in bereavement overload. We need to come to a better understanding of what we can do to help. Death and dying have to become a community responsibility, not just the province of the nuclear family or the duty of next of kin.

We need to have knowledge about end-of-life choices embedded in the general community, so that it is no longer taboo to talk about what we feel and think about our own deaths and the deaths of those close to us. How we care for our dead and dying is an expression of the spirit of a society. Ignorance, isolation, and fear will make the last years of the Silver Tsunami (baby boomers) a difficult time for the country, a time of misery and mourning, rather than a celebration of how this cohort has shaped our culture and a moment in which we reap the benefits of their wisdom and express our love

There is no way to spare ourselves sorrow, but there are many things we can do to avoid regret. As a dying person, we can take hold of the freedom inherent in letting things go, talking about what is real and true, doing the things on our list that need doing, and finding a way to die that suits our own sensibilities and the needs of those around us. As a family member we can work to bring our family together around a death, rather than tear it apart with conflict over how to handle the stress and the resources. As a friend, we can offer comfort and support without judgment, learn patience and presence, and exercise courage. As a community, we can make a place for those who are dying and those who are mourning that encourages empathetic responding, emotional safety, and spiritual support, as well as the best medical care. As a country, we can find time to remember and grieve our losses, respecting the past as we continue to rush toward the future in a fast-paced, complex society.

References for This Chapter:

Morgan, J. D. (1993). The existential quest for meaning. In K. J. Doka & J. D. Morgan (Eds.), *Death and spirituality* (pp. 3-10). New York, NY: Baywood Publishing Co.

Noel, B., & Blair, P.D. (2008). *I wasn't ready to say goodbye.* Naperville, IL.: Sourcebooks, Inc.

Seligman, M.E.P, Schwartz, T., & Bennis, W. G. (2018). *On mental toughness.* Cambridge, MA: Harvard Business School Publications (see the interview on post-traumatic growth by Martin Seligman).

Seligman, M.P.E. (2012). *Flourish: A visionary new understanding of happiness and well-being.* New York, NY: Free Press.

Further Reading

Ariés, P. (2008/1982). *The Hour of Our Death: The classic history of Western attitudes toward death over the last one thousand years.* New York, NY: Vintage Books. (Original work published 1982.)

Bush, N. E. (2012). *Dancing past the dark: Distressing near-death experiences.* Pennsauken, NJ: BookBaby.

Byock, I. (2012). *The Best Care Possible.* New York, NY: Avery/ Penguin books.

Cameron, J. (Producer), & Psihoyos, L. (Director). (2018). *The game changers* [Motion picture]. United States: ReFuel Production, Oceanic Preservation Society, Diamond Docs.

Capra, F., & Luisi, P. L. (2014). *The systems view of life: A unifying vision.* New York, NY: Cambridge University Press.

Corry, J., & Wendel, B. (producers), & Fulkerson, L. (director) (2011). *Forks Over Knives.* United States: Virgil Films and Entertainment.

Hagan, J. C. (2017). *The Science of Near-Death Experiences.* Columbia, MO: University of Missouri Press.

Holden, J. M., Greyson, B. E, James, D. E. (2009). *The handbook of near-death experiences: Thirty years of investigation.* Santa Barbara, CA Praeger Publishers, pp. 63-86.

Holloway, M. (2002). *Negotiating death in contemporary health and social care.* Bristol, UK: University of Bristol Policy Press.

Isbouts, J.-P. (2016). *Ten Prayers that changed the World: Extraordinary stories of faith that shaped the course of history.* Washington, DC National Geographic.

Jenkinson, S. (2015). *Die Wise: A manifesto for sanity and soul.* Berkeley, CA: North Atlantic Books.

Kastenbaum, R. (2004). *On our way. The final passage through life and death.* Berkeley, CA: University of California Press.

Kübler-Ross, E. (1969). *On Death and Dying: What the dying have to teach doctors, nurses, clergy, and their own families.* New York, NY: Simon and Schuster.

Moreman, C. M. (2010). *Beyond the Threshold: Afterlife beliefs and experiences in world religions.* New York, NY: Rowman & Littlefield Publishers, Inc.

Ornish, D. (2008). The spectrum: a scientifically proven program to feel better, live longer, lose weight, and gain health. New York, NY: Random House Digital, Inc.

Ostaseski, F. (2017). *The Five Invitations: Discovering what death can teach us about living fully.* New York, NY: Flatiron Books.

Patel, R., & Moore, J. W. (2017). *A history of the world in seven cheap things: A guide to capitalism, nature, and the future of the planet.* Oakland, CA: University of California Press.

Pollan, M. (2009). *In defense of food: An eater's manifesto.* New York: Penguin Books.

Robert K. & Pearlstein, E. (producers), & Robert K. (director). (2009). *Food, Inc.* United States: Magnolia Pictures.

Shiva, V. (2016). Who really feeds the world? The failures of agribusiness and the promise of agroecology. Berkeley, CA: North Atlantic Books.

Sousa, J., & Staudt, C. (2009). *The many ways we talk about death in contemporary society.* Lewiston, NY: The Edward Mellon Press.

Wulf, A. (2015). *The invention of nature: Alexander von Humboldt's new world.* New York, NY: Knopf.

ABOUT THE AUTHORS

JUDITH STEVENS-LONG, PhD

Dr. Stevens-Long has served as a professor and Malcolm Knowles Chair for Adult Development and Learning in the PhD program in Human and Organizational Development for Fielding Graduate Institute. She has been a professor and administrator in higher education for over 40 years at Fielding Graduate University, California State University and the University of Washington, where she was a founding member of the faculty at the first branch of UW in Tacoma. At Fielding Graduate University she designed one of the first online master's degrees in the country.

Dr. Stevens-Long has extensive experience as an organizational consultant as well as a professor and administrator. She has specialized in communication and team-building and has worked with professionals in the fields of law, medicine, and university education. She has published numerous books and articles in adult development including four editions of the best-selling text *Adult Life*, where she first began writing about death and dying. Her recent publications include articles on grand theory in human development, personality and ego-development, the assessment of graduate education, and the design of virtual educational environments. She has recently completed the second edition of the Oxford bibliography in Adult Development.

Dr. Stevens-Long lives in Santa Barbara with her husband, Larry, where she serves as a volunteer for the Hospice of Santa Barbara and enjoys being the parent of adult children and the grandmother of three lively granddaughters and one grandson.

DOHREA BARDELL, PhD

Born on a Kibbutz in Israel, Dr. Dohrea Bardell was raised with egalitarian principles that formed the foundation from which she frames her life and work. Her PhD research in Human Development and International Relations culminated in the design of a Kantian normative theory for peace. She has presented her theoretical model at various peace and international relations organizations, including The International Studies Association (ISA), the Peace & Justice Studies Association (PJSA), and the International Leadership Association (ILA).

One of Dr. Bardell's long-time passions is the study of large world theories and the influence they exert on the way scientists organize and explain life, health, and death. As a Fellow at the Institute for Social Innovation, Dr. Bardell has joined Dr. Judy Stevens-Long to research the process of death and dying. Their book, *Living Well, Dying Well* is modern, data-driven, enlightening, and down-to-earth practical.

For over 30 years, Dr. Bardell has straddled both the biological and the social sciences, working in the integrative medical community as well as researching diverse social issues, from the health status of nations to the state of world peace. Together with her husband Seann Bardell, she has taught holistic health, consulting corporations, healthcare providers, and individuals on healthy lifestyle practices. Her nutriceutical company, BioImmersion, works in partnership with a global network of scientists, manufacturing experts, farmers, and physicians to design innovative food supplements.

Appendix 1

A Living Will

TO MY FAMILY, MY PHYSICIAN, MY LAWYER, MY CLER-
GYMAN, TO ANY MEDICAL FACILITY IN WHOSE CARE I
HAPPEN TO BE, TO AN INDIVIDUAL WHO MAY BECOME
RESPONSIBLE FOR MY HEALTH, WELFARE OR AFFAIRS:

Death is as much a reality as birth, growth, maturity, and old
age—it is the one certainty of life. If the time comes when I,
_____(legal name)_____

Can no longer take part in decisions for my own future, let this statements stand as an expression of my wishes, while I am still of sound
mind.

If the situation should arise in which there is no reasonable expectation of my recovery from physical or mental disability, I request that
I be allowed to die and not be kept alive by artificial means or "heroic measures." I do not fear death itself as much as the indignities
of deterioration, dependence, and hopeless pain. I, therefore, ask that
medication be mercifully administered to me to alleviate suffering
even though this may hasten the moment of my death.

This request is made after careful consideration. I hope you who
care for me will feel morally bound to follow its mandate. I recognize that this appears to place a heavy responsibility upon you, but
it is with the intention of relieving you of such responsibility and of
placing it upon myself, in accordance with my strong conviction,
that this statement is made.

Signed _____

Date_____

Witness_____

Witness _____

Copies of this request have been given to

name_____

name_____

name_____

Source: Euthanasia Education Council of New York

Made in the USA
Middletown, DE
29 September 2018